# ONLY HUMAN

## SIMPLE STEPS TO RESHAPE YOUR LIFE

ANNA VEALE

First published by Ultimate World Publishing 2022
Copyright © 2022 Anna Veale

ISBN

Paperback: 978-1-922828-75-0
Ebook: 978-1-922828-76-7

Anna Veale has asserted her rights under the Copyright, Designs and Patents Act 1988 to be identified as the author of this work. The information in this book is based on the author's experiences and opinions. The publisher specifically disclaims responsibility for any adverse consequences which may result from use of the information contained herein. Permission to use information has been sought by the author. Any breaches will be rectified in further editions of the book.

All rights reserved. No part of this publication may be reproduced, stored in or introduced into a retrieval system, or transmitted in any form, or by any means (electronic, mechanical, photocopying, recording or otherwise) without the prior written permission of the author. Any person who does any unauthorised act in relation to this publication may be liable to criminal prosecution and civil claims for damages. Enquiries should be made through the publisher.

**Cover design:** Ultimate World Publishing
**Layout and typesetting:** Ultimate World Publishing
**Editor:** Isabelle Russell
**Photographer:** Salina Galvan Photography

Ultimate World Publishing
Diamond Creek,
Victoria Australia 3089
www.writeabook.com.au

# Tribute

To my dad, you are always with me.

To my mum, thank you for all the little things and the big things too.

# Testimonials

Anna is that rare blend of a driven and inspired human who has managed to stay connected to her heart. All the passion she has for living life finds its expression in a unique ability to empower others to bring forth their very best in any area of life they chose. As a highly skilled and insightful coach, Anna is always one to walk the talk and, as such, you can rely on her expertise to be tried and tested.

**Josh Roche, High Performance Coach**

Anna's approach is a wonderful blend of both life experience and scientifically proven methods. Her natural warmth, personality and passion, alongside a wealth of knowledge of both body and mind make up one truly fantastic coach. It has been my pleasure to know and work with Anna for the last 20 years. *Only Human* is a fascinating and practical insight into self-improvement and her formula MENS is the result of many years of practice with clients, who have achieved amazing results. Anna has a knack of making complex topics understandable and relatable and wherever you are now, you can 'start where you are'. A pleasure to read.

**Stuart Leonard, High Performance Coach**

# Contents

| | |
|---|---|
| Tribute | iii |
| Testimonials | v |
| Foreword by Henry Fraser | ix |
| Introduction | 1 |
| 1 Why MENS? | 7 |
| 2 Upgrade Your Mindset | 19 |
| 3 Is Your Mind Full? | 37 |
| 4 Values – Your Playbook For Life | 49 |
| 5 Beliefs | 65 |
| 6 Stress | 71 |
| 7 Exercise | 103 |
| 8 Nutrition | 123 |
| 9 Sleep | 151 |
| 10 Bringing It All Together with Ayurveda | 165 |
| 11 It's in Your Hands | 179 |
| Acknowledgements | 185 |
| References | 187 |
| About the Author | 189 |
| Access to Free Resources | 193 |
| Offers | 199 |

# Foreword

## Henry Fraser

There are few people you meet in life like Anna. She is awesome, for all the best reasons.

I believe in the good in everyone and few personify it as Anna does. I know of almost no one who can connect with people as quickly or as deeply as her. She genuinely cares and genuinely listens, absorbing everything. Generous with her time, her love and her compassion.

Anna's experience as a personal trainer and massage therapist for professional athletes and teams has brought her in contact with people at all stages of their wellness journey and they have benefitted from her infectious enthusiasm and positive outlook. I have always been competitive and up for a challenge; I work just that little bit harder and push myself that little bit further.

Anna shares these traits and that makes her uniquely placed to help people to achieve their goals. As part of my recovery, from an accident that left me paralysed from the shoulders down in 2009, I found that "the art of striving gives meaning".

Only Human

In the same spirit, Anna has set up programmes coaching people on how to manage stress and make positive changes to their lives.

I rarely get the joy of seeing Anna as much as I used to, but each time we talk it's so easy, like the time we haven't seen each other never existed. This is all down to her because she is so welcoming and genuine- a really honest, genuinely good person.

I am sure you will connect with what Anna has written in the following pages and that you will find *Only Human* an engaging read.

**Henry Fraser**
**Mouth artist**
**Author of *The Little Big Things* and *The Power in You***
**Motivational speaker**

None of us knows when we will take our last breath, so it is my mission to motivate as many people as possible to live their lives with passion, intent and heart, so their relationships are strong, connected and purposeful.

# Introduction

I was lucky enough to grow up in a household with a dad who, I knew, loved me no matter what. He was a kind and thoughtful man who loved his family more than anything else in the world.

In many ways, he was ahead of his time. He had healing hands, an incredible mind and a unique gift of making every person he encountered feel like the most important person in the room.

Like all of us though, he was only human. And he was a human who drowned his demons with booze.

He would often sit and ruminate on the things he hadn't done, could have done and wished he had done. The drink would make him melancholic, and he blamed the world and his bad timing for missed opportunities.

Like many people battling addiction, to the outside world, he was engaging, fun to be around and full of life. At home, though, especially in the last ten years of his life, he was in physical and mental discomfort, which slowed him down considerably.

## Only Human

During my personal training career, I saw too many people living half-lives, chasing a dream which wasn't even theirs, always running on a metaphorical treadmill, *Groundhog Day*, different people, but the same feeling – unfulfilled. Now, when I work with people in my coaching practice, I provide a safe container to throw ideas around and give them the tools to safely and confidently step off the treadmill and take full ownership of their lives.

None of us knows when we will take our last breath, so it is my mission to motivate as many people as possible to live their lives with passion, intent and heart, so that their relationships are strong, connected and purposeful.

This book gives you the power to see things through a different lens and change the habits of a lifetime. This is a book of action. I'll be asking you to take daily, positive steps so that a year from now, you can look back and see how your life has improved exponentially in just 365 days.

Time and time again, I have seen the pressures you are under and the beliefs that stop you from having fully connected relationships with yourself and the people who matter most in your life. The great news is: We have the answers within us, and with a little bit of work, the simplest of steps can have a profound effect on life as you know it.

I've seen individuals like you go from being stuck and grumpy to creating time for themselves, finding their fun, playful side, being more attentive and interested at home, changing their work circumstances, taking control of their health and making time to see their friends again. These are all results of their dedication to changing their mindset and having the courage to take control so they can reshape their lives for the better.

## Introduction

I challenge you to adopt the same mindset as my clients and ask yourself the hard questions that you've been too scared to answer, so you can become the person you truly want to be.

I don't know where you are at in your life right now. Perhaps you are a few kilos above your fighting weight, or you know you drink a couple more beers than you should, but it helps you relax after a big day. Maybe your partner has noticed that you're being distant or too focused on work because you can't switch off when you're at home. What about the guy that cut you off at the roundabout? Did you smile at him and let it wash over you or did it wind you up to boiling point?

This book provides you with the basics. Simple steps that will increase your self-awareness, but more than that, encourage you to take the action required to positively change your life. In return for making that commitment to yourself, you will find a renewed sense of energy, more intimacy with your partner if you have one, and you will feel more deeply engaged with life.

I'll take you through my easy-to-follow MENS framework (MINDSET, EXERCISE, NUTRITION and SLEEP) and together we will fix common problems like having no energy, limited time, lack of intimacy or living a high-stress, reactive life.

Throughout our journey in this book, you will be given exercises to strengthen your commitment to the lifestyle changes you choose to make. You will hear stories of people who have been in similar situations to you and changed their lives for the better, by implementing some of the strategies outlined on these pages. Note that for privacy reasons, I have changed the names of some of my clients.

You can use the dedicated sections within this book to record your findings or head over to http://www.freshcoaching.me/onlyhumanresources to download my *Only Human* companion workbooks.

This isn't a book that you read and forget about. Use it as your playbook for daily life-a benchmark of where you are now and where you will be in just a few weeks if you put the work in. Refer to it often and use it as your anchor when you feel yourself veering off track. This book will help you work through your blind spots, unlocking your true nature so you can live the life you were born to live.

Change is hard – that's why most people don't bother. They stick to their habits and blame their environment for not being in the place they want to be. But you're not like that. You are someone who wants the best of what life has to offer, and to attain that, you are going to have to put your excuses to one side and give me your A-game.

Are you ready? Let's go.

When life gets easier, your relationships get stronger.

When life gets easier, you stop looking externally for happiness.

When life gets easier, you connect deeply to what matters to you.

When life gets easier, you have more life to live.

# 1

# Why MENS?

If you were given a process that could take you from where you are now to where you really want to be, would you use it?

In my coaching practice, I train clients through the simple framework, MENS, to move them from feeling average to incredible. This framework is made up of four essential pillars: MINDSET, EXERCISE, NUTRITION and SLEEP.

I developed MENS after training and coaching hundreds of people throughout my career. If one of the four pillars was out of whack, it had a rolling effect on the other, which in turn greatly affected the quality of their lives.

When we pay attention to each of the four pillars, life gets easier.

When life gets easier, your relationships get stronger.

When life gets easier, you stop looking externally for happiness.

When life gets easier, you connect deeply to what matters to you.

When life gets easier, you have more life to live.

Take Matt, for example. Matt was a client of mine whom I trained back in the early 2000s. On the surface, he was a highly successful businessman with a beautiful family and a large social network. Matt was the owner of a successful international business and his family lived very comfortably. When we met, he was clearly exhausted, 'wired', frenetic almost. Every morning he left the house in the early hours, usually racing out of the door without having eaten and grabbing a coffee on the way to the office. His day would consist of fighting fires, answering emails, closing deals and managing his team, before realising he was late for a dinner appointment, social engagement, school event, or most Monday nights, his training session with me!

When I talked to Matt about the type of life he wanted, he couldn't articulate 'what' exactly, but that he just knew the treadmill he was on wasn't it. I was personal training Matt at the time and his 'goal' was to lose weight. It was evident that thrashing him in the gym was not going to work long term. Together, we formulated a game plan to get him focused on the long game. It was imperative to get him in the right headspace. To achieve this, we zoomed out so we could look down at his life and get a clear view of the hamster wheel he was trapped on. Only then was he able to see the negative cycle he had created for himself in the pursuit of success.

When we zoomed out, he noticed what an automatic, habit-driven life he led.

## Why MENS?

As soon as he opened his eyes, he was in work mode. Like most people, he used his phone as his alarm, which then prompted a habitual pattern of opening his emails before he'd even greeted the day. After a shower (during which he was occupied by work thoughts), he would get dressed and bolt out of the door, ready for his fast-paced corporate day. Having skipped breakfast and relied on caffeine to keep him alert, he would either meet clients for lunch or grab convenience food and eat at his desk before feeling shattered mid-afternoon, then drink more coffee which would keep him going until he burst through the door at 6:30pm.

Like many people his age (mid-40s), he was greeted by the usual chaos of his excitable children who wanted to spend time with him and his partner (who was ready to hand them over to him so she could have some time to herself) or, as mentioned, race into other evening commitments while apologising for being late. This same pattern, day in, day out, along with other evening commitments, left little, if no, time for Matt to check in with himself. Over time, this way of living wore thin. His capacity for tolerating even low-level stress reduced to the point where he found himself using alcohol to relax in the evenings, often falling asleep on the sofa, having missed important connection time with his partner.

Once we established that this wasn't what Matt wanted long-term, his mindset shifted, and his energy changed. Suddenly, he could see that his behaviours weren't reflecting his values (which we will cover in an upcoming chapter) and by making a few conscious choices, his life could be very different.

With his head in the game, we worked on sharpening his mindset. I gave him easy mindfulness exercises to do throughout the day, including noticing his triggers, witnessing his thoughts and actions, creating space between those thoughts and reactions and becoming conscious of his unconscious behaviours.

We agreed on easy habit-changing actions when it came to his exercise, eating and sleeping. We made the changes so simple that he couldn't skip a day. Over the course of time, *he* became his own biggest project and the results spoke for themselves. His family said he was more attentive and less grumpy. His work rate was still high and effective *and* he reached his goal of losing weight.

By following MENS and creating his own formula, to this day, Matt gained and has maintained his newfound energy and zest for life.

Matt is just one example of the many people I have worked with, who have become so focused on one important area of their lives (namely work) that they lose sight of the bigger picture. If this resonates with you, then you are going to enjoy diving into the MENS framework. If you follow the process I'm about to set out for you, you will undoubtedly look and feel better. Your outlook on life will be different and you will be able to consistently be at your best.

MENS isn't about denying or depriving yourself of the things you enjoy. I'm not going to ask you to shave your head and move to the Himalayas to become a monk, or to become a vegan Crossfitter, who sleeps in a futuristic sleep tank. In fact, I'm not going to tell you how to exercise, what to eat or when to sleep. What I am going to ask you to do is check in with YOUR mind, YOUR body and get deeply connected to YOUR constitution so that YOU can build a deeply personal WHY to bring about YOUR transformation.

## MENS

### M = MINDSET

With around 60,000 thoughts per day, most being the same as yesterday, the week before and the year before that, most of us are living on autopilot. Building an aware, resilient and flexible mindset is essential to elevating our day-to-day lives. You are going to learn how your beliefs deeply shape your current reality and how to give yourself an upgrade so you can see your life through fresh eyes.

It helps to know that our brain naturally leans towards the negative, constantly on the hunt for danger, primed to keep us safe. This outdated mechanism in our brain reduces our ability to 'be positive' which serves us well when under threat, but severely takes the edge off living a contented life if we rely on it. Becoming aware of this default setting in our mechanics is powerful stuff, as you will find out later.

Without a healthy mindset, you aren't going to get far in reaching your definition of happiness. It requires a shift in state and dedication to creating positive energy that aligns with your values and goals for life. It's about having an awareness of self that can be firm yet compassionate, focused yet vulnerable.

This awareness can be learned through mindfulness. Being mindful is a vital tool to develop because it gives you ultimate power. In the sweet spot between stimulus and response, quite literally lies the capacity to change your life.

When we move away from stress and towards our values, life gets easier. Learning the importance of values and identifying what matters most in your life will give you freedom. They will help you navigate through life in an authentic and powerful way, and work as an anchor for when you're pulled in different directions. With this clarity, you can set meaningful goals and take positive, intentional action to bring about the change you desire.

Improving mental fitness not only deepens your connection with yourself, but it also frees you from the confines of your mind, strengthens relationships and creates connection and purpose within your partnerships instead of becoming distant and incompatible over time.

In 2020, 103,592 divorces were granted in England and Wales, 7,707 in New Zealand and 49,510 in Australia. Although each couple no doubt had their own reasons, I am willing to put money on the fact that the demise of the couples' relationships started with a lack of communication and instead, plenty of miscommunication, which led to a change in behaviour over a period of time, resulting in divorce.

It is my strong belief that we can reduce divorce rates by focusing on strengthening our mental fitness and taking good care of ourselves so we can create a solid foundation for relationships to thrive. By being the change we want to see, we can protect our relationships whilst honouring our own identity.

**E = EXERCISE**

For far too long, Western culture has led us to believe that our body and mind are separate entities, but when one isn't performing, it's hard for the other to be at its best. The most successful athletes work on their mindset and the most brilliant minds move their body, in some way, shape or form, during their working week. Exercise doesn't mean thrashing yourself in the gym or becoming the next iron man contender – it simply means moving your body consciously

## Why MENS?

every day. I have met too many guys who have dropped out of sport when they became busy at work and had a family to return to in the evening. Not only did they lose the fitness component, but they also lost the social aspect, which are both vital for wellbeing. It's important to find a suitable replacement to keep the body active whilst maintaining social interaction.

Be honest with yourself: How much time do you spend outdoors in the fresh air moving your body? Many of my clients leave the house early on their commute to work, go from the car straight into the office, then from the office back into the car, back home, dinner, couch and bed.

Research suggests that being outside for 20 minutes, three times a week helps to boost cognition and memory as well as improving your overall sense of wellbeing. Personally, I get a lot of my inspiration for writing when I'm outside. In the exercise chapter, we will cover how to integrate more outdoor time and movement and dial down on how to link it to your values, so that the time you schedule for movement doesn't get bumped off when something 'more important' (like a work call or email) comes up.

**N = NUTRITION**

Have you ever tucked into a takeaway after feeling like you were 'starving', inhaling the food without giving it enough time to touch the sides only to feel absolutely 'stuffed' half an hour later? Your sides probably felt like they were going to explode, and you might have felt tired and lethargic for some time afterwards. Or perhaps you're like Matt – too busy to eat, so you eat on the run, in the car, at your desk or snack on cheese, crackers and a wine in that dead time before dinner is ready.

In this chapter, we will prioritise your eating habits over exactly what you are eating. Identifying habits that don't align with fuelling your body will play an important role in creating long-term, sustainable change. Not only that, but you will also find that you can still eat and drink the foods you love *and* reach your health-related goals.

**S= SLEEP**

A few years ago, I was lucky enough to attend a seminar by All Blacks' strength and conditioning coach, Nic Gill, who talked about optimising performance in sport a few years back. He discussed the key areas of an athlete's life that needed to be addressed for the players to show up at their best on game day. Sleep, he said, was the top priority. Getting good quality sleep, consistently, will dramatically improve the way you show up to yourself and others.

Getting a good night's sleep isn't just about getting eight hours; it's about taking positive steps from the moment you wake up to ensure the quality of your sleep is optimal. It's about making choices that align with sleeping well. By resetting your circadian rhythm, you are creating a pathway that guarantees a good night's rest. In this book, you will be equipped with well-researched tools you can incorporate into your daily routine that will have you sleeping like a baby and waking up with energy and optimism for your new day.

You can see that my simple MENS formula empowers you to take easy, proactive steps that over time create a compound effect resulting in a powerful and purposeful life. This process is perfect if you're feeling stuck, in a negative cycle and are ready to step up and change.

Following are two circles. The one to the left is where you're at currently. The one to the right is to use to mark your positive

## Why MENS?

progress in 12 weeks' time. Remember that you can go to http://www.freshcoaching.me/onlyhumanresources and download the exercises.

In the first circle, shade in the areas where you currently sit for each of the MENS. Be completely honest about how much time you spend getting these fundamentals right on the daily. If you have let any of the areas slip down the list of priorities, you aren't alone. Simply colour in the proportion of time you currently spend taking care of each element. In an ideal world, all four areas would be completely shaded. There's no need for excuses or blame; simply notice where you're at.

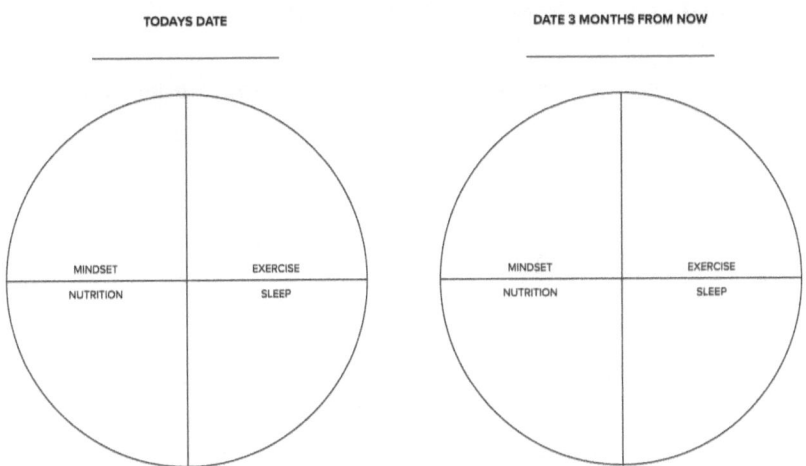

Use the following chapters to build your knowledge, relate to the stories I share and inspire you to step up, take control and reshape your life.

## SUMMARY AND ACTIONS

- Your life is your responsibility.

- You hold the key to change your life.

- Simple changes make a huge impact. Start small and build over time.

- Make time every day to work on your MENS.

- Download the companion workbooks by visiting http://www.freshcoaching.me/onlyhumanresources.

- Complete the first MENS circle to get your benchmark.

**First comes awareness, then comes change.**

# 2

# Upgrade Your Mindset

Optimum mindset is the root of it all, and, because of that, this is where we are going to spend most of our time together. I've broken down this meaty chapter into several parts that all deserve their time in the spotlight.

**Would you date you?**

We are going to start where your head is at right now. If we were together having a chat, what would I notice? Would you be confident? Engaged? Interested? Relaxed? Joyful? Would you be calm, present and balanced? Or would you be doubtful? Distracted? Nonplussed? Tense and serious? Would you be thinking about the next meeting in your diary?

Pay attention to how you answer those questions and then ask yourself if that's how you commonly interact with your family, friends or at work. Perhaps certain people in your life trigger more negative behaviours than others. Perhaps your cup is so 'full' that when someone asks something of you, it seems too much and you react negatively. Or maybe your mind is so overloaded that it's preventing you from being fully present.

One misconception when I'm working with people is their belief that once they change something in their external world, their lives will be better. Once they get the credit card paid off, they will feel calmer. Once they finish the big project at work, they will have the time to spend on their family. Once they finish the household renovations, they will eat food that fuels them. The reality is, that there will ALWAYS be something that's going to take you away from the important things in your life, so it's down to you to build a solid routine whereby life happens AROUND the things you hold dear to you.

Back in 2020, around eight months after COVID hit, my mental health declined. The world as we knew it changed and, although I was taking good care of myself physically, I dived into my work. The face-to-face aspect had all but dried up and I was left, like thousands of others, having to pivot my business. Originally from England, I left a very loving family and tight friendship group to live our dream life by the sea in New Zealand. After a few months of the pandemic, it became apparent that I wasn't going to be able to get home anytime soon and that caused my mental health to decline further. Whilst on the outside I was fully functional, on the inside I was hurting. On 10 February 2021, my 43rd birthday, My son Jack wrote me a birthday card which read *'Five facts about Mum'* Number three was, 'She cries a lot.' Reading that hit me like a bullet and was the hit that I needed.

As a coach, I had all the tools to help me, but I had missed one vital piece. I had allowed external events to shake my core and I was giving the pandemic all my power. I had become a victim to circumstance. Instead of practising being 'in the now' (which is hard work and takes discipline, patience and practice!), I spent time worrying if I'd ever see my elderly mum again. I became distant from my husband and kids and created all sorts of awful scenarios in my head which left me feeling helpless and deflated. Sitting there, on my birthday, reading that card, I realised that something had to change. I promised myself I would take 100 per cent responsibility for the things that I could control and learn to let go of the things I couldn't.

That card was pivotal for me. I became focused and directed, like a laser beam. I stopped watching the news. I asked my friends and family to only give me information on COVID that impacted us directly. I used the time that we couldn't travel to deepen my meditation practice, by booking the ten-day vipassana retreat that I had been putting off because my 'Anna only' time was always spent going home to England for a week every year.

I took total control of my life. I looked at the implications of moving back to England, considered closing the business down and getting a job that required less energy and concluded that my foundations were solid, but I had just allowed myself to become a victim. On that day in February, everything externally was the same, but my mental state changed and that made me see my life through fresh eyes.

Our mindset changes throughout the day. Between the stimuli we receive, (information from our internal and external world) and our responses to them (our reaction to that information) we have a tiny window in which we can choose a different response. Most of our responses are automatic responses which makes them hard to change. But with self-awareness and practice, you can catch yourself before you react and change your state and the outcome.

Can you think of areas in your life where you blame your circumstances for not being where you want to be? Perhaps you feel your boss isn't giving you the recognition you deserve, or your co-workers aren't performing. Or perhaps you don't feel understood at home? Maybe it's even wider than that. The government? COVID? Now, look at how much energy you expend and the physiological responses in your body in reaction to the stress. Living life by taking 100 per cent responsibility isn't easy. When I took on the challenge, I realised just how much of myself I gave away to others, and how many excuses I made for my life being the way it was. The irony of that was, I consider myself to be mostly optimistic and grateful. But when I zoomed in, I noticed just how much I allowed circumstances to stop me from living.

Edith Eger, a survivor of the horrific death camp Auschwitz, discusses in her book, *The Choice,* how she overcame the most unimaginable trauma and near-death experience. During her ordeal, she was made to dance for the Nazi officers, was moved to multiple camps, walking long distances with no food, suffered malnutrition and was barely clothed. She was left to starve to death before American soldiers found her amongst a pile of bodies, when they liberated the camp in 1945. Despite the trauma she endured, she never gave up hope and was determined that although the German soldiers could strip her of most things, they could never take her mind.

The following powerful quote from *The Choice* reinforces the fact that our strength of mind comes from within regardless of the external circumstances. I hope it will serve as a reminder that when you decide to take responsibility for your life, you can overcome even the most distressing of circumstances.

*'Victimhood comes from the inside. No one can make you a victim but you. We become victims not because of what happens to us but when we choose to hold on to our victimisation. We develop*

*a victim's mind through a way of thinking and being that is rigid, blaming, pessimistic, stuck in the past, unforgiving, punitive and without healthy limits or boundaries. We become our own jailors when we choose the confines of the victim's mind.'*

## SUMMARY AND ACTIONS

- Regardless of how hard it seems, we always have a choice.

- Taking 100 per cent responsibility is the hard choice but it is incredibly empowering.

- It is easy to blame the world but there's no room for happiness if you choose to stay living below the line.

- Acceptance of 'what is' empowers us to drop blame and victimisation.

- Notice how often you blame external factors for your circumstances.

- Watch out for excuses you make for the areas in your life that you want to improve.

- Take positive, intentional action to change these habitual patterns.

- Make a habit of creating distance between the stimulus and response. It's remarkable when you find that sweet spot, time slows down and you are given a moment to choose a different, more values-aligned response.

## Are you stuck?

Have you ever wondered why it's easier to be in a bad mood than a good one? If you answered 'yes', then you aren't alone. Our subconscious mind is primitive. We are hardwired to lean towards the negative. As humans evolved, this was a useful mindset to have because it kept us on high alert for danger. It was useful to keep us safe from threats, other tribes, wild animals and deadly environments. Being able to respond to these threats kept our species alive. The downside to that, however, is that our brains haven't evolved as much as the world around us has, and whilst we are unlikely to be eaten by a bear anytime soon, this genetic human trait affects how we think, feel and respond in this new modern environment.

So, how does this negative bias keep you stuck? This natural tendency unconsciously seeks out potential danger and risk, which in turn plays a part in your decision-making ability. Tom, one of my first coaching clients, was a hardworking, intelligent man who came to me when he had hit rock bottom. He was working for a difficult boss who had unrealistically high expectations, minimal leadership skills and was 'old school' in his approach to management. Logically, Tom knew that he was a good worker. He was conscientious, loyal and went the extra mile to do a good job, but the constant negativity from his employer was wearing him down. Tom felt undervalued, micromanaged and stuck. His relationship had taken a knock because of his stress levels, and by the time he came to me, his whole life was falling apart.

When I asked him what his strengths were, his confidence had taken such a hit that he couldn't think of any. When it came to his relationship, he talked about the areas that weren't going well. In fact, every area of his life that I enquired about came back with the same response: 'Well below average.'

## Upgrade Your Mindset

Tom was stuck in his own negative feedback loop, and he didn't have the capacity to see the wood for the trees.

As part of the onboarding process, when I take on a new client, I ask them to complete a questionnaire that provides me with information about their challenges and way of thinking, so that when we start our sessions, we can make them purposeful and achieve results. Luckily for me, I knew that Tom had done some pretty cool things in his past, so when I probed for more details about these, his entire demeanour changed, and for a moment, he could see that he had a lot to offer the world. Within a matter of weeks, he had found a new job, entered and commenced training for a half marathon and stepped away from his relationship. A year later, I reconnected with him, and he told me his life had changed exponentially. His new boss was a dream to work for and he was earmarked for promotion. His improved fitness had led to his taking better care of his basic needs of nutrition and sleep and he was in a promising new relationship.

Tom is a prime example of somebody who got caught in a web of negativity. Everything he saw was distorted and that had a knock-on effect on other aspects of his life. I'm sure you've had days where one thing went wrong for you and no matter what you did, for the rest of the day, drama and pain seemed to follow you. This is a less severe example of how we can get drawn into the negative cycle and emotional pain becomes our reality.

The worrying thing about being in this negative loop is that it's very difficult to get out of. What we see is what we attract. Like attracts like. It takes strength and courage to recognise it and pull yourself out.

Let's try an experiment. Scan the room you're in currently and notice all the grey in it. Look around you, in front, behind, up above and down on the floor. Observe all the grey you can find. When you've done so, close your eyes and recall all the blue that's in the room. Don't take a sneaky peek or the experiment is void!

How did you get on? Most likely, you couldn't recall many blue items – if any. This is a prime example of how our brain sees what we pay attention to. If you have an area of your life that's not going so well and your focus is on all the things that are wrong, the chances of you seeing the slightest bit of positivity are highly unlikely.

The negative bias isn't all bad though. In fact, it is vital for our survival, as it's how we learn. Our threats are very different now to caveman times, and they are much less likely to kill us. Like most things, once we have an awareness, we can choose how to respond accordingly.

Our brain is a very clever machine. To make sense of the millions of bits of information it receives every day, it uses a filter system to take on board information that's important and let's go of the rest. These mental shortcuts are essential and very helpful. We don't have to think about tying our shoelaces, brushing our teeth before going to bed or taking a shower. Where it can be difficult in life is when we have unnecessary negative responses to situations in our lives. These responses are often automatic, habitual and fly under the radar. These negative thoughts, otherwise known as negative automatic thoughts (NATs), come from our childhood. We all have unconscious conditioning from our upbringing which form our thoughts and beliefs about the world. If we don't stop to ask ourselves if these beliefs are real, then the thoughts will go unnoticed and will ultimately control how we feel and react to life.

To get your head around what I'm talking about, I'll give you an example of one of my NATs and the resulting negative impact it has, not only on me, but on my family, if I don't keep myself in check.

## Upgrade Your Mindset

I grew up with a mum who loved to travel. Her teaching career took us away to Europe on school exchanges and trips. As much as she loved to spread her wings, I remember the build-up to these trips being stressful. She and Dad would raise their voices at each other. The energy of the house was frenetic and, from a child's perspective, the days before we went away were clouded with stress, distraction and unease. On the occasions I travelled with Mum, she would be preoccupied organising her students – she rarely had time to take a breath. It wasn't until we were in the air that she would settle.

The pattern was the same when we went on family holidays, the build-up of tension in the days leading to our trip and the big breath out once the plane took off and we were on our way.

I grew up assuming that stress before travelling was normal, so, as an adult, I carried on the tradition of getting highly strung, unconsciously mimicking the behaviour of my parents. I would feel the tension build in my body, probably making it quite awkward for the friends who were coming with me, in the days leading up to travel. Once I learned about NATs, I realised that my response could be different, that I could reframe the situation and create a new 'pre-travel reality'. If I consciously thought about how exciting the build-up to the trip was, creating new rituals and beliefs, I could break the habit and cut the cord on the NAT.

Don't get me wrong, when I travel, the sneaky NAT tries to creep back in, but so long as I've kept myself mentally and physically well, I usually have the resilience to catch it, reframe and get back on track, breaking a pattern that could have been passed down from generation to generation.

This diagram of the cognitive behavioural therapy (CBT) triangle will help explain how our thoughts trigger our feelings, which affects our behaviour and how the pattern continues if we don't think to question our thoughts. CBT is a therapy used to help people understand their thoughts and feelings so they can become 'unstuck'.

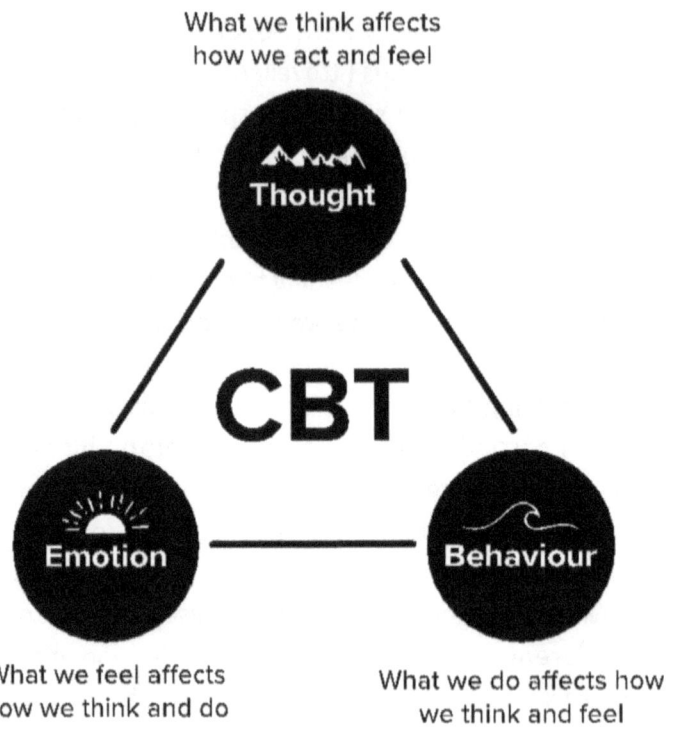

Once we build awareness, we have the power to challenge our thoughts and question their validity. Rather than accepting thoughts as facts, we can choose whether to believe them. This is different to suppressing emotions and sweeping them under the carpet. It's vital that we acknowledge and sit with uncomfortable thoughts and feelings, so they can pass through quickly and move on to more helpful, values-aligned action.

## Thought overhaul

Language is powerful, not only for the people we talk to, but how we talk to ourselves. It's a primary tool to express ourselves and communicate so tuning into the way we talk, both internally and to others, can shed light on how we really think and feel. Have you stopped to listen to the thoughts that play on repeat in your mind, or are you too busy with life to notice? If you have ever tried meditation, you might be one of the thousands of others who have been surprised at how much their brain had to say! Noticing our repetitive self-talk and listening to the way we respond to others will help change the way we show up in life. The unconscious mind does most of the driving, and most of us have an unhelpful voice that, if left unattended, puts the brakes on us living a calm and balanced life. All-or-nothing thinking can turn a small situation into a tsunami of pain.

When I'm facilitating workshops, I like to use the unanswered email as an example.

Picture yourself at work: you're under the pump, with balls flying in from every angle. You are pretty tapped out and your body is on high alert. You fire an email out to a supplier and have the expectation that it needs to be replied to immediately.

Ten minutes go by, you refresh your emails and there's no reply. Maybe you phone him, no reply. You can feel yourself getting frustrated, but crack on with other jobs, with a niggling story in your mind about how frustrating the supplier is.

Half an hour goes by – still no reply. The voice inside your head is getting louder now as you create an elaborate story about how he's always letting you down, that the service isn't up to scratch, and you must make a note to check out other suppliers in the area.

A couple of hours on, you've moved your story to, 'I wonder what I've done to upset him? Why isn't he picking up my calls? Perhaps it was because I didn't use him for that job last time.' Then you swing back to contempt: 'Prick. If that's what he thinks, then I won't bother using him next time.'

The day goes by with no answer to your calls or your email and you have started getting snappy with your co-workers. You are distracted and don't have patience for the people who require your immediate attention. Your partner calls and you are distant and non-communicative. That causes them to feel like you're upset with them, or worse, they feel you don't care about what is going on for them at that moment. You start stomping around. The story of the incompetence of the supplier has been blown into a full-on movie and your frustration has turned into anger.

At 5:30 pm, you check your emails and there's a reply from the supplier. 'About time,' you mutter to yourself, ready for a gunfight.

You open the email.

'Hey, I'm sorry it's taken so long to get back to you. My daughter had an accident and I had to drop everything and take her to the hospital. She's OK, but it's been one heck of a day. Here's the quote, I hope the delay hasn't set you back too much. Give me a call if you want to discuss anything in more detail.'

Ouch. I think we have all experienced similar moments.

Perhaps when you were dating and sent the first text message to your new love interest. You knew they had read it, but they hadn't replied yet. Our brain loves to make meaning from things, so no doubt you had thoughts such as:

- 'They must not like me.'
- 'What's taking them so long to reply?'.
- 'What did I say or do that might have upset them?'.

Before you know it, you have spent your day stewing over a completely made-up event that often is so far from reality.

Our ego loves to be right and will go on a mission to find the evidence to match the reality that exists in the mind. It's our job to step out of our ego and take an observer's view, so we can see the bigger picture.

Once we learn the skill of creating space, stepping back and observing before jumping in, we have the power to see the whole landscape instead of what's just in front of us. This skill alone can dramatically change relationships and help us to overcome obstacles that otherwise seem impossible to move through.

How we talk to ourselves directly translates to how we show up in the world. If there are areas in your life that aren't going your way, it would pay to look inwards at the way you're treating yourself. Positive self-talk isn't arrogant or cocky. It helps promote confidence, problem solving and resilience. Negative self-talk, on the other hand, can damage self-worth, affect relationships and reduce your overall quality of life. Whilst there will be occasions where we don't talk to ourselves in a respectful way, catching the thought and unhooking from negativity will help change the way we see ourselves in the world.

In the process of writing this book, I've had moments of waking up in a panic, worrying that I'm not good enough and that people won't like what I've written. The thoughts seemed so real, in the moment, which triggered feelings of anxiety and fear. I naturally lean towards being quite hard on myself, so it was easy for me to fuel the story that I don't have the skills or knowledge to be an author.

Luckily, through the art of awareness, I have taught myself to unhook from the unhelpful thoughts, acknowledge that it's fear that's driving them and move towards my wider goal. Acknowledging unhelpful thoughts and feelings takes the power out of them. Accepting they aren't helpful, and most likely aren't true, gives me the power to act (in this case, continue to write despite the negative chatter), which, in turn, gives me confidence to crack on with the mission!

If we can break the reactive cycle and become a bystander to our thoughts, we can start to break down NATs that are holding us back from living life to the full.

## SUMMARY AND ACTIONS

So, now you know about the negative bias and how natural it is for us to fall into it, here are some simple action steps to pull you out of that default negative pattern.

- **First comes awareness, then comes change.**

We can't change what we don't know and the message throughout this book is going to be the same. Awareness is king. Now you know where the negative bias comes from and why we have it, you can look for where it appears in your life and watch it from a distance.

Ask yourself if the negative thought you're having is true, and if it is true, is it helpful?

Believe it or not, your thoughts aren't real. We can't control the thoughts we have, but we can decide if they are true and if they are useful.

- **Negative bias is necessary for survival, but not always helpful.**

Challenge your default thought pattern by looking for the good in the situation.

- **What are your NATs?**

How can you catch and reframe them so you have a positive outcome for the future?

- **Distance yourself from negativity.**

Like attracts like, therefore negativity breeds negativity. If you are going to consistently change your mindset, it would be wise to remove negative influences from your life as much as you can.

- **Energy vampires.**

Energy vampires are the people in your life who drain your energy when you spend too much time with them. Distancing yourself from people who constantly complain, blame, judge and compare will supercharge your energy stores. Encounters with energy vampires are draining and rarely result in positive outcomes. It's difficult to remove people from your life, I get that, but at the very least, acknowledge who depletes you of energy and manage the time you spend around them.

- **Limit watching and reading the news.**

If you are someone who reads, listens to or watches the news, I highly recommend you limit yourself to tuning in once a day, a few hours away from when you go to bed and not when you are eating. News is rarely full of joy and positivity, and our nervous system doesn't need the overload of bad news that the media portray 24/7. This one habit change can make a massive difference to your attitude and is one of my non-negotiables with clients.

- **Watch out for your own negative energy-thieving habits.**

Remember that habits can so often fly under the radar, so you must actively look out for them and consciously take steps to change them. This is hard work in the beginning because it takes effort. Stick with it, the results will be worth it.

We are what we repeatedly do. To have an optimal, directed and engaged life, consistently skipping workouts, eating poor quality food and not taking responsibility for your health will catch up with you.

Spend a few days dialling into your unconscious habits. Where does your time go? What food are you eating without realising? How many drinks do you put away despite thinking you've only had one or two? How many times do you pick

## Upgrade Your Mindset

up your phone and not engage with your partner or kids when they are right in front of you? How many times a week do you fall asleep on the couch, only to wake up cold and disorientated? How often do you press the snooze button every morning? All these unconscious habits add to the negative load on the body and mind.

The pace of life isn't going to slow down. Your to-do list is still going to be as long as your arm and there will always be something else that requires your time. So, unless you change your perception, life will always feel full, with little or no room for joy.

# 3

# Is Your Mind Full?

I'm aware that mindfulness is a buzzword, and you might be tempted to skip this chapter; however, I encourage you to read on. Once upon a time, I, too, would have rolled my eyes and told you that I was too busy to sit on the floor and focus on my breath! But then I came to understand the true power of mindfulness.

The pace of life isn't going to slow down. Your to-do list is still going to be as long as your arm and there will always be something else that requires your time. So, unless you change your perception, life will always feel full, with little or no room for joy.

Mindfulness is the skill that might just give you the space to see the richness of life that stands before you each day.

It has been said that we are human beings, not human doings. There's a reason we have been given intelligence and a soul. Mindfulness teaches you to step off the treadmill and choose a different way of living, with less doing and more being.

Meditation is the vehicle to help you bring more mindfulness into your life. In the pages that follow, you will learn the difference between the two and have the opportunity to experience the benefits for yourself.

## Mindfulness

Mindfulness is the basic human ability to be self-aware on a physical and mental level, whilst remaining detached from the thoughts and feelings we experience in a given moment.

When we learn mindfulness, it allows us to become aware of thoughts, and then create space between those thoughts and consequent actions, giving us a window of opportunity to choose how we respond to a situation, rather than reacting habitually.

Mindfulness encourages flexibility and curiosity instead of rigidness and judgement, which, in turn, gives us the freedom to make decisions that align with our values, rather than being trapped in a miserable habitual cycle of stress.

You can practice mindfulness anywhere. Over time, you will be able to quickly observe negative thoughts and patterns and consciously make corrections and positively move forward.

The downside to 'waking up' and living mindfully, however, is that pain will undoubtedly arise. Pain from your past, fear of the future and moving beyond the habitual patterns of your mind. It takes awareness and a true commitment to the bigger picture to stay on course.

Mindfulness is bringing consciousness to the unconscious mind and that requires discipline, commitment and time.

## Meditation

Meditation is a practice. It is a learned skill that you build on, which offers a medium to obtain more mindfulness in your everyday life.

Meditation is mostly a sitting or lying practice and there are hundreds of different styles and philosophies that surround this ancient art.

From the yogis to the military, meditation is a skill that asks you to sit with courage, lean into your reality and be accepting of what arises in that moment.

As mentioned, I initially found both mindfulness and meditation to be a waste of time. I believed that if I wasn't thinking, then I wasn't being productive. If I didn't 'jump in the fire' to help my friends and didn't feel deeply, I wasn't a good friend. I believed that life was too short to sit still, and I glorified 'busy'. To me, a still mind meant a dead mind. How wrong I was!

In 2013, my world was spun on its head when my father died suddenly. My whole life, I had been 'preparing' for his departure from this world. He was 45 when I was born, and I grew up with a fear that he wouldn't see past my 16th birthday. The irony was that he lived longer than he anticipated, witnessed his children grow up and have their own families, and although I had spent decades waiting for the call, I still wasn't prepared when it came.

There's nothing quite like the experience of losing a parent. When it was my turn to say goodbye, I felt an emptiness that has stayed with me ever since.

Logically, you can rationalise death, and well-meaning people say things like, 'He had a good innings,' 'At least he died quickly,' 'You're lucky you had 36 years with him,' 'It's the circle of life,' but on a deeply emotional level, no amount of logic can move you through the grief you find yourself in.

In the weeks after his death, I would find myself staring at the ceiling in the middle of the night, unable to sleep with thoughts racing through my mind. I'm sure you've had nights when you can't sleep and every tiny thought snowballed into catastrophe, leaving you restless and stressed.

In those moments, the darkest of my life so far, my mind felt scrambled and my emotions were extreme and unrelenting.

One night, a few weeks after I had returned to my home in New Zealand from England where my family were, I googled 'mindfulness for beginners' and stumbled across an app called *Headspace*. The host, Andy Puddicombe, was from England, so I was immediately drawn to his voice and message of developing mindfulness with just 10 minutes of practice a day.

Although I knew my head was full of crazy, exhausting thoughts, when I sat down to do one of Andy's meditations for the first time, I was shocked by how much noise was in there! He talked about focusing on my breathing and encouraged me to notice when I had become hooked on a thought and moved away from the breath. When the mind took me away, Andy said, 'Just label it 'thought' or 'feeling' and gently come back to the breath.' I'm not exaggerating when I tell you that I lost count of how many times I had to pull myself back!

That first experience proved just how much noise was in my head and how much work there was to do.

## Is Your Mind Full?

As the days and weeks passed, I continued my commitment to 10 minutes of meditation a day. In that time, I learned how to allow the grief to move through me.

The time I spent in meditation offered me the chance to slow my brain down, to give it a rest and reset. The outcome meant I was less past- and future-oriented, and I was more connected to the people and things that were right in front of me. I was able to sit with the overwhelming thoughts and feelings and let them wash over me, instead of being swept down the river with them.

Beyond the grief, I learned so much about myself – how I was living life on autopilot without the awareness and skills to break free from the confines of my mind. What also surprised me was how many times I used food, exercise and work as a distraction from my feelings.

Off the mat, meditation gave me the freedom to create a new reality. I became less reactive; I spent less time ruminating and could unhook from negative states more quickly.

What I found was that I was resistant to letting go of the grief. My ego was committed to the belief that if I let go of the pain, it meant I didn't care about my dad. The pain that I had was so connected to the love that I felt for him, that to let go of it left me cold. This took quite a long time to unpack, but by doing the work, I realised that, again, it was a pattern I had created throughout my life. To show I cared about a person, situation or thing, I developed strong attachments and a deep connection between pain and love. Consistent meditation and constant vigilance to my hardwired, conditioned patterns eventually broke a very strong belief that changed how I saw and reacted to the world. Powerful stuff!

Mindfulness and the practice of meditation literally changed how I saw the world, and, as a direct result, my life changed for the better. It didn't happen overnight, and it required constant commitment. Being mindful and raising awareness links back to taking 100 per cent responsibility for our life, the way we perceive it and how we show up to it. Meditation is the vehicle to fast-tracking our body and mind to get us to that place of peace.

Here's the lowdown on what it could do for you. Mindfulness allows you to:

- Let go of the conditioned stories created by your past experiences
- Accept life as it is rather than what you want it to be
- Step back from the reactive habitual responses you have to life
- Live in the present
- Challenge thoughts and 'choose again'
- Unhook from repetitive thoughts and stories
- Self-regulate
- Release old trauma

Meditation brings you:

- Time for yourself
- Time to reset
- More applied, focused living
- Detachment from negative emotions
- Improved physical health
- Improved mental health
- Peace

## Is Your Mind Full?

Acceptance and commitment therapy uses values and mindfulness to help people build purposeful lives. It stands on six core principles; values, Committed action, diffusion, acceptance, 'self as concept' and committed action. Whilst I won't write too heavily about the therapy itself, its model aligns with my style of coaching. Weaving in mindfulness gives us the freedom to step away from the ego and make better choices for our lives. It makes room for doubt in our 'must be right' minds, which allows us to take different actions. It gives us permission to unhook from habitual stories and identities that we created for ourselves, years ago, and aren't who we are now. It creates space for inner peace and harmony.

When I work one-to-one with people, unless they have experienced meditation before, it's quite far down on my list of tools. Mindfulness, however, is a priority.

The moment people experience the space between stimulus and response, their lives change. Mindfulness creates a tiny window of time that has life-changing capabilities.

As a personal trainer, one of the areas I was interested in was people's eating habits – what they ate, when and why. I consistently noticed resistance to keeping a food diary. They would usually say they had forgotten, or it was too hard and took too much time. When they got over the initial pain of completing it, they realised how much food and drink they were consuming, unconsciously, and could see the real reason they weren't reaching their weight loss goals.

Mindfulness is about cultivating an awareness of all the 'thought food' you are consuming that holds you back from getting the life results that you want.

Change must start with awareness. Once we establish that, we can apply choice. Once we apply choice, our life changes exponentially. Becoming aware gives us the freedom to choose again. The freedom to unhook from habitual conditioning that keeps us stuck.

Over time, using mindfulness with the help of meditation, we can begin to build new habit patterns, which disengage our habitual, unhelpful thoughts.

Once this happens, our life improves. We can look back at periods of our lives where we weren't acting in accordance with our values and understand that, at that moment, we did the best we could do, but now we know better our response to a similar encounter will be different.

The bottom line is: Living a mindful life will show you very quickly the areas in which you are resisting reality. It will highlight the people and situations that trigger your inner peace, giving you the space to choose a different behaviour in response to that stimulus, empowering you to live life above the line. Living mindfully will change your perception of the external landscape, giving you the power to live life on your terms.

## Gratitude – Misery's Achilles Heel

There's a reason that coaches, thought leaders and Buddhist monks put time into gratitude. It's because it's the kryptonite to negativity: misery's Achilles heel.

If you don't already know him, I want to introduce to you an extraordinary human, Henry Fraser. I don't say that just because he's my friend, but because of the heroic way that he adjusted to life after experiencing a serious accident which left him paralysed from the neck down. Whilst I could write about him all day, I wanted to use him as an example of what real gratitude looks like and how it can dramatically alter your mood.

After Henry's accident, there was a long period in which he and his family had to adjust to the new reality. One of Henry's coping mechanisms was to focus on what he was grateful for in his life. In our conversations, he talks about how having an appreciation for the things in life that we would ordinarily take for granted, is a huge mood enhancer, from the taste of a cup of tea to the kindness others showed him. Spending time deeply appreciating the little things made a positive impact on his recovery and mindset.

When we go through difficult periods in our lives, it can be difficult to see beyond the pain we are experiencing in the moment. It can also feel like finding things to be grateful for is a waste of time in comparison to the strong feelings we are going through. But in every dark moment, there is something, somewhere, if you look hard enough, that gives you peace in the moment.

When my dad died, I spent a month in England. My daughter was 18 months old at the time and in my darkest hour, my little girl's eyes got me through. She had this lovely habit, when she was going to sleep, of snuggling up face to face and staring into my eyes, whilst simultaneously playing with my hair. In the days after Dad's passing, we lay in my old bed, cuddled up, nose to nose, sharing these deeply grounding moments. As she slowly drifted off to sleep, I felt a deep sense of gratitude that has lasted over a decade.

Gratitude, to me, is about having an emotional feeling about something I can deeply appreciate in the moment. As Henry said, it's usually the little things. The smile from a passing runner, the stars in the sky, the first cup of tea in the morning. I've noticed the things I'm most grateful for are the things that I most take for granted. The quantum moments with the kids, the cold glass of water my husband throws at me whilst I'm enjoying a warm shower, the sun rising as I finish my morning exercise. Truly, it's the little things.

I guess what I'm saying is to be careful not to use gratitude as a 'have to do' exercise. Look out for the little things, those moments that might otherwise pass you by. Look for the feeling because when you do, you will experience the positive effects that stay with you long after the moment has passed.

So, how can you be grateful without it becoming a 'shopping list', or just another thing to add to your to-do list for the day? Whilst there are endless ways to feel gratitude, here are some ideas that might inspire you.

A few years ago as a family, we decided to start dinner by saying the three things that went well or we enjoyed during the day, and one thing that could have gone better. This ritual now serves as a primer for good conversations and learnings. It's become such a family tradition that we rarely skip a night! Interestingly, the kids always talk about the things I most take for granted. Things like dinner, exercise and hanging out with their mates.

When you think of someone – your parents, a mate or work colleague – let them know. Send them a text, or better, give them a call. This tiny act will not only have a positive impact on your mood, but it will also brighten their day too. Win-win!

Look for the good. Our brain tends to delete, distort and generalise, to make sense of the world. It bends the truth to fit our beliefs and

## Is Your Mind Full?

map of the world. Look for the good in situations and your mental landscape will change.

Write down what you deeply appreciated from your day, before you go to bed, and ask yourself a question like, 'How can I bring more joy/discipline/connection into my day tomorrow?' Close your eyes and go to sleep. Your unconscious mind is like a loyal dog and will go and find your answer. When you know what helpful questions to ask the mind, and you ask them consistently, the magic starts to happen!

Check in and take yourself back to a good memory. Notice the shift in your physiology. Who was there? What were you doing? Bring the memory back to life. Hold it. Notice the creases of your mouth moving upwards and your shoulders dropping down. Stay with it for as long as you can, then bring yourself back to the present moment and soak up the positive energy you have just created for yourself.

From a scientific perspective, practising gratitude helps to release the feel-good hormone, dopamine, the very hormone that is released when you eat food that tastes good or when you reach for the alcoholic drink you associate with relaxing after a tough day. This release of hormone is so powerful that it leads you to wanting more, which, when we are looking at living with gratitude, could well be where your future happiness lies.

Gratitude helps you pull up the weeds of negativity that may be growing in your mind. By regularly practising appreciating what you do have, there will be less room for drama cycles and more space for inspired thoughts.

To be honest, I think we could all do with a little of that, don't you?

Values will give you the roots and grounding required to weather the storm that life throws at you.

# 4

# Values – Your Playbook For Life

To live a life with energy, vitality and passion, it helps to know your values. Once you have got clear on the values you want to live your life by, it becomes your very own playbook for life.

Your playbook will allow you to set boundaries for yourself and others. It will give you the freedom to be yourself *and* can be used as a benchmark for how you're treating yourself and others.

This chapter is going to teach you what we should have been taught at school. Values are worth more to me than Pythagoras' theorem ever was!

As you know, our spirit is constantly being tested so when you know what deeply matters to you, you'll find the power to honour your way of life amidst all the challenges.

Values will give you the roots and grounding required to weather the storm that life throws at you.

In essence, values are our deepest aspiration for how to be our best selves. How we show up to ourselves, other people, our work and our life. They represent our strongest selves, what we stand for, and act as a compass to come back home when we stray off the path.

Values are different to goals. They form the basis of how to 'be' so you can create, strive for and achieve your goals. They are intangible. They can't be taken from you, and they are deeply personal. Values get us out of bed on the cold, dark mornings when we would prefer to press snooze. They help us choose hard over easy when faced with dilemmas, and they help you find your tribe when it comes to relationships. Values can change as we change, and we may find ourselves prioritising some values over others. There will also be times when your values are compromised and you find yourself feeling stuck. When you do, you'll be able to refer to this chapter to work your way through it with minimal drama.

Values are:

- Deeply personal to you
- A compass to guide you through life
- A healthy code to live by
- Motivating
- A strong companion for reaching high-end goals
- A way of bringing true meaning to the reason you're here!

Values are not:

- Tangible (apart from family)
- Goals (they support you in building strong, congruent goals)

## Values – Your Playbook For Life

- Set in stone (they can change and evolve)
- A list of random words that sound good but don't resonate deeply with you
- Beliefs
- Chosen for you by someone else

So, how do we go about finding our values and creating our own playbook for life?

Like tracking our thoughts, if we take time to look at the areas of our lives where we are in flow and peace *and* the areas of our lives that create heat and passion, we will likely be led to uncovering our values.

When we are deeply connected to our values, we lose track of time, our body language changes, we become open, passionate and expressive. We are aligned. We are free.

Can you think of some examples in your life in which you lost the concept of time and felt deeply connected to what was going on? Perhaps at a sports event, a friend's wedding or when you started your own business? What was it about that example that had you suspended in time? What qualities were you displaying and how did you treat yourself and others?

Connection is something I deeply care about: connection to self and others. I LOVE football and have been to see my team, Arsenal, play multiple times over the years. The atmosphere at Highbury and, in recent years, The Emirates, is always electric. The stadium welcomes 60,000 strangers, united together with one goal: To win.

The interesting thing about my love of the game is my inability to recall the results. I remember the feeling. The unity. The connection.

## Only Human

I watch the sport for those reasons, and yes, in the moment it's brilliant to get the ball in the back of the net, but for 90 minutes, I'm connected to the people around me. For 90 minutes, they are my tribe.

Conversely, can you think of a time when you were triggered by something, and it sparked something inside of you that you wanted to defend?

As a young teenager, I went on holiday to the stunning island of Mallorca with some family friends. It was my first holiday away from my parents and I was loving the sense of adventure and freedom that came with the trip. I had known my friend's family since birth. They were generous with their time and welcomed me to their holiday home with open arms.

One afternoon, my friend and I joined her uncle for a game of tennis. Having grown up as the youngest of four siblings (younger by a square mile!), I was deeply competitive and held strong values of hard work and fairness. As the tennis match went on, it was evident he was doing his best to beat me, which is fair enough, but I grew more and more frustrated with the comments he was throwing my way. Well-meaning but unhelpful remarks like, 'Come on, what's the point of playing if you're not going to try,' put my back up more, and I eventually lost my cool, threw my racquet to the ground, told him exactly where he could shove it and stormed off the court back up the lonely streets of Puerto Pollensa, back to the safety of the villa.

This is a prime example of how I felt my value of hard work was being questioned and how, regardless of the consequences, I would defend it.

## Values – Your Playbook For Life

In many ways, finding what matters most to you gives you the freedom to be who you want to be, rather than the person you think you should be for society, family and friends. Perhaps you have grown up with the belief that happiness and success come when you go to university, get the corporate job and have the big house. You go along with it because you don't want to stand out from the crowd or disappoint your parents, but you feel discontented and out of alignment. Or maybe you drink too much because you believe it's the social thing to do, when really you would prefer to enjoy just one or two.

Beliefs and values can be confusing and until we start raising our awareness of our thoughts and behaviours, it's too easy to live a life of outdated beliefs that don't align with the life you want to live. Beliefs are assumptions that we make about the world around us based on our upbringing, past experiences and other influences. Beliefs are often true for us, but not for others. They can move us forward, but equally they can hold us back if they are false and outdated.

Values are directly related to our needs and can shape our identity from the inside.

When you're clear and deeply committed to living by your playbook, you can more easily set boundaries for your life. And when you are going off course, like we invariably do as humans, we use the playbook to guide us home.

The big question to use to find your values is WHY? When we ask that question, we connect straight to our emotional brain. This part of the brain is responsible for decision-making and controls behaviour. Hence, asking 'WHY'? will get you to the values that matter to YOU. This part of the brain will give you the real answer, instead of the answer you feel obliged to write down to fit in with your peers or family.

Below are a couple of exercises that will help tease out what matters most to you. As you work through the exercises, imagine that I'm next to you asking, 'Why? What is it about what you've chosen that matters to you?' When you have your answer, ask yourself the same question. You might do this a few times before you drill down your true value.

If your head is buzzing, don't worry! You're only human! This is big stuff. Big stuff that matters! Once you become clear on your 'WHY', life becomes so much more fulfilling!

Whilst there are hundreds of exercises to find what matters most, here are a couple of my favourites that I use when working with clients, one-on-one:

> This exercise has been taken from Russ Harris' book *ACT Made Simple*.
>
> Most of us have either seen or heard of the movie *Castaway*. Tom Hanks' character gets stranded on a desert island after being involved in a plane crash.
>
> Imagine this is you, stuck on a remote desert island, with your family and friends back home holding a funeral in your honour.
>
> A few weeks later, you're rescued and fly home to a happy reunion. Sometime later, you get the opportunity to watch a video of the funeral.

## Values – Your Playbook For Life

As you are watching, you listen to a handful of the people you love the most talking about your life.

What would you love to hear them say about:

- The sort of person you are

- Your greatest strengths and qualities

- The way you treated them and made them feel

Make some notes here:

_____

_____

_____

_____

_____

_____

_____

_____

Below is a non-exhaustive list of common values.

Look and reflect on the words, highlighting any that deeply resonate with you. Once you have done this, trust your gut and choose your top four.

LEGACY / SIGNIFICANCE / ENERGY /

FREEDOM / ACHIEVEMENT / RECOGNITION /

TRAVEL / FAME / BELONGING /

KNOWLEDGE / SELF ACTUALISATION /

UNIQUENESS / FAIRNESS / CAREER /

FAMILY / FAITH / KINDNESS / HEALTH /

LOVE / DETERMINATION / BALANCE /

WEALTH / HAPPINESS / SUPPORT /

EQUALITY / COMMITMENT / FRIENDSHIP /

COMMUNITY / SPIRITUALITY / INNER PEACE /

PURPOSE / SECURITY / CONTENTMENT /

SUCCESS / RECOGNITION / / COMFORT /

FINANCES / INDEPENDENCE / DECISIVENESS /

CHALLENGE / DISCIPLINE / NATURE /

## Values – Your Playbook For Life

INSPIRATION / FINANCIAL FREEDOM / VISION /

ENVIRONMENT / FRIENDS / POWER /

AMBITION / PROFESSIONALISM / RESPECT /

JOY / STRUCTURE / BEAUTY / VARIETY /

CREATIVITY / STABILITY / TOLERANCE /

BOLDNESS / PATIENCE / CALL TO ACTION /

CONTRIBUTION / DIVERSITY / FAITH /

COOPERATION / LEARNING / COMPASSION /

GENEROSITY / INTIMACY / INSPIRE /

COURAGE / EXCELLENCE / FRUGALITY /

GRATITUDE / FUN / MINDFULNESS /

DEPENDABILITY / DISCOVERY / EMPATHY /

ENCOURAGEMENT / GROWTH FLEXIBILITY /

HOPE / INTEGRITY / INTUITION /

OPTIMISM / PASSION / RESILIENCE /

TRUST / OPENNESS / ORIGINALITY /

PERSUASIVENESS / SACRIFICE / SIMPLICITY

Now that you have your top values, write down what they mean to you personally and how you will behave so you live in integrity with them.

VALUE 1: _____

What it means to me:

_____

_____

_____


How I will live in integrity with this value:

_____

_____

_____


VALUE 2: _____

What it means to me:

_____

_____

_____

# Values – Your Playbook For Life

How I will live in integrity with this value:

_____

_____


VALUE 3: _____

What it means to me:

_____

_____


How I will live in integrity with this value:

_____

_____


VALUE 4: _____

What it means to me:

_____

_____

**How I will live in integrity with this value:**

_____

_____

_____

**Let's go deeper:**

**Ask yourself:**

**What is taking me away from living a life that is true to my values?**

**Who do I need to become to live by these values?**

_____

_____

_____

## Values – Your Playbook For Life

What will be my identity? What habits, behaviours and actions will help align me to living with this playbook for life?

_____

_____

_____

How can I apply these behaviours in my life right now?

_____

_____

_____

Who will benefit from these changes?

_____

_____

_____

Once you have completed those two exercises, you will be well on your way to changing the way you show up to life. Taking positive daily actions from the information you have gathered will bring you one step closer to fulfilment.

## What to do when the stars collide

It is tempting to think that once you have established your values, life will become easier. No matter what, there are going to be times when our values conflict and it leaves us feeling unsure of how to respond.

My brother is deeply committed to his health and his family. At work, he is loyal, hardworking and disciplined. He puts his heart and soul into any project he's given. These qualities have made him hugely successful at work. Because of these values, he quickly became the guy that you could rely on 24/7. The colleague that would not only get the job done, but ahead of time and with exceptional quality.

When the children were little, he and his wife decided to move away from the hustle and bustle of London so the kids could have freedom, outdoor space and be closer to family. The downside was that his workplace was still in the city, a three-hour train commute away. Some days, he would leave the house at a gruelling 4:00 am to tackle the commute and be at his desk in time for 8:00 am kick-off. He has always kept himself incredibly fit and, over time, despite his unwavering positivity, the long commute started to take its toll.

The limited time he had with his family was spent amidst a fog of tiredness, and, despite his best efforts, his energy dwindled and his health started taking a hit. At that time, his values of family and health were being sacrificed at the cost of his other values, loyalty and hard work. On top of his fatigue, his energy was even more depleted by his feelings of guilt and pressure. At times, he felt like he couldn't give his best in either camp. This is a prime case of conflicting values.

Maybe you have been caught in a similar situation. Perhaps you value integrity and career and you're offered a promotion without having to go through formal procedures. Your value of getting ahead in your career now conflicts with integrity being at the heart of what matters most.

Maybe you value health and connection. One of your friends loves going for big nights out, so you go out and spend time with him and spend the rest of the week feeling out of sorts as a result.

The fact is, there will often be conflicts in life. It's just about being conscious enough to acknowledge when they occur and working out a game plan that is congruent with your lifestyle at the time. My brother soon realised he valued his family and health over the constant demands that city life threw at him, so he chose to make a change in career closer to home which he still works hard at and excels in, but now has the time to put into his family and health.

Humans are meaning-making machines.

Beliefs are not the truth. Beliefs are our perception of the truth.

# 5

# Beliefs

A word on values versus beliefs. Values bring meaning, importance and purpose to your life. A belief is an assumption we create based on our own map of the world. Beliefs are not the truth. Beliefs are our perception of the truth. There is a big difference and understanding this concept will help change the way you see your life.

From birth, we absorb information and feedback from our caregivers and those around us. Lacking experience and wisdom, we take on tones of voice, body language and encounters and make meaning out of it. An innocent remark from a kid in the playground can cement an unconscious belief that gets reinforced over time. A poor grade in a maths test can take on the belief that 'I'm rubbish at maths,' which later limits us in business and finance. Beliefs are unconscious and because of this aren't questioned or challenged, and many of us are being held back by our outdated belief system being triggered by situations, and we don't know why. Uncovering limiting beliefs changes how we see the world, relationships and ultimately our lives.

## Only Human

I grew up believing that men and women should have separate bank accounts and keep their finances totally separate instead of forming a financial partnership. When my husband and I had children and moved to Australia, we were fully dependent on his salary and my belief that I should be financially independent was challenged. It took a lot of work for me to get my head around the fact I had to rely on his salary during that time, and it caused my behaviour towards him to change. When he asked me a question related to money, I automatically got defensive instead of seeing it for what it was: an innocent day-to-day question!

Let me explain further. My dad was an incredible human. He was kind and generous. He made every person he met feel loved and acknowledged and he was engaging and funny. People loved him. I loved him. When he was drunk, though, he was unpredictable. Sometimes he was on great form and lovely to be around, but more often he was argumentative and had a vicious tongue.

Because of his unpredictable behaviour, I grew up very wary of people who drank a lot and although of course I went through a phase in my teens and early twenties of having a few too many, I often found myself feeling uncomfortable in social situations where there was a lot of alcohol.

This unconscious belief made me hypervigilant, and for a few years it really messed with my head.

My belief that good people who are amazing to be around when sober have the potential to be awful when they are drunk is based on my experience and although it may be 'true' for me, it doesn't mean it's true for everyone.

## Beliefs

So, why does it matter? In my case, my behaviour changed. My belief that all people were awful when they were drunk made me look out for the evidence for it to be true. I would often pick a fight with my boyfriend or get the hump if people were having fun back at the house and I was trying to sleep. I'd get anxious about going out to a party, wedding or the pub and throw some sort of tantrum a couple of hours before I was due to go. To outsiders, I would have looked like a diva – high maintenance and unreasonable. For decades, I didn't understand this behaviour either, but since I've done the work, I can see that my brain was doing its best to keep me out of danger. Drunk people equal danger.

Now that I've given some examples from my own life, can you look under the bonnet and notice beliefs from your upbringing that might be outdated, holding you back and simply not true?

(Beliefs relating to finances, relationships, your intelligence or looks). What messages were you given from well-meaning caregivers? What sweeping statements are holding you back from having the life that you deserve?

- 'I'm not worthy of being loved.'
- 'I'm too old.'
- 'I don't have enough money.'
- 'That's just for rich people.'
- 'I've never been good at sport.'

Recognise your limiting beliefs when they arise and be alert. Hunt them out. Compassionately and curiously question their validity. Identify where the belief first came from. Is it true? Give the belief a positive reframe.

For example:

'I'm not good enough to go for the promotion.'
Is the statement true? (No, you aren't the one conducting the interview!).
Where did the belief that you aren't good enough come from?
Where's the evidence to suggest you aren't good enough in the present moment?

(Usually, there won't be, and if there is, then that's what you can work on to get the skills required to go for the promotion.)

Positive reframe:

'I'm going to apply for the promotion and prepare without putting an expectation on the outcome.'

(Positively reframing and acting without making the outcome of the interview mean anything about you, as a person.)

When you notice old beliefs running, it's your opportunity to call them out, change your behaviour and move toward your values. When you start living this way, your outlook on life will change and you will create a new reality for yourself.

You will find a beliefs meditation in your bonus resources:

http://www.freshcoaching.me/onlyhumanresources

Create some time in your day where you won't be disturbed to download and listen.

Human suffering is natural and normal. It is not to be shied away from or thought of as a failure in some way.
– Josh Roche, Performance Coach

# 6

# Stress

According to Mental Health UK, a recent survey suggests that 74 per cent of people have been so stressed and overwhelmed that they felt unable to cope. While 46 per cent of those people reported to eating unhealthy food and 29 per cent turned to drinking alcohol to deal with life stressors.

In New Zealand, information gathered from the Mental Health Foundation indicates that 14 per cent of the population will be diagnosed with depression at some time during their lives.

These alarming statistics demonstrate just how much chronic stress is stripping us of our happiness and wellbeing. Stress, however, isn't the enemy. It's how much of it and for how long, our tolerance and responses to it that determine whether it is friend or foe.

Before we hammer this misunderstood condition, let's look at why, in the right context, stress can keep us safe and elevate our performance.

Stress has undoubtedly garnered a bad reputation over the past couple of decades and whilst chronic stress can take years off your life, stress itself can save it! Have you ever had a heart-stopping moment when you've stepped out onto the crossing, only to find the car isn't going to stop, so you jumped back on the pavement? What about the time you accidentally left the hob on, and you smelt burning coming from the kitchen? Without your brilliant stress hormones, you might have been hit by a car or missed putting the fire out from your burned baked beans!

Low-level, short-term stress is necessary for optimal performance. Getting nervous for the interview for your dream job, building the courage to ask the person you like out on a date or the day you drive your newborn baby home from the hospital. In these examples and countless others, stress serves a purpose and can help us survive AND thrive.

A little stress is natural. It helps you to meet everyday challenges and keeps your mind sharp and goal focused. Stress used in the right context can become a good friend.

Chronic stress, not so much. It is your utmost responsibility to take this section seriously and take measures to adapt to your internal stressors so you can live the life you deserve!

Chronic stress comes with problematic symptoms such as:

- Headaches
- Loss of libido
- High blood pressure
- Muscle tension
- Anxiety and depression
- Digestive disorders and constipation

- Weight gain
- Insomnia
- Isolation and withdrawal from the things you usually enjoy
- Tiredness and fatigue
- Lack of focus and inability to concentrate
- Burnout

The list above includes just some of the by-products of stress. It's no wonder that stress has been labelled the biggest cause of disease, stealing the joy from our lives. Even if you present with only one or two symptoms from the above list, your ability to live life with energy and passion is still significantly reduced.

I've noticed from both my own experiences and those of my clients, stress can creep up on us, making it hard to prevent, but as I said at the beginning of this book, you can do hard things and when you do, your life will be richer for it.

## Physiology of stress

It helps to know what happens to our bodies on a physiological level so you can identify your responses to stress and start to shift out of the red zone so you can live life to the full.

When our brain perceives that it is under threat, it releases hormones called adrenaline and cortisol into the body, to prepare for battle. These hormones, triggered by the sympathetic nervous system, increase our heart rate and elevate blood pressure to help us fight, run or freeze. Our brain has no way of knowing the difference between physical stress and psychological stress, so when our stress response is constantly triggered by fast-paced lives, rather than these hormones shutting up shop for the day, they continue to work overtime. As a result, our body becomes overloaded with stress hormones and our health suffers.

These important hormones serve a vital role in our existence, but our brain hasn't evolved enough to recognise when we have a real threat (getting hit by a car) or a perceived threat (being late for work). The same hormones are produced and pumped around the body, but whereas you would use them to power you up to quickly get out of the way of the vehicle, they flood the body when you're stuck in traffic, leading to frustration and anger.

The long-term effects of chronic stress don't bode well for relationships, work satisfaction and happiness. If your body constantly thinks it is under threat, you will be unable to make rational decisions in accordance with your values. You'll restrict your ability to set meaningful goals and be so depleted that you'll miss the little things that count.

## Psychology of stress

Stress occurs when our reality, real or perceived, doesn't match the expectation in our minds. Think about it: The areas in your life you feel most wound up about are the areas you think should be different. Someone at work isn't pulling their weight, the kids are always trashing the place, your partner is too tired, and there isn't enough time in the day. It all comes down to one thing: our resistance to accepting reality as it is.

Although I understood the concept, it wasn't until I experienced 10 days of a monk's life at a vipassana retreat in 2021 that I felt it on a deeply personal level. Vipassana means 'to see things as they really are'.

## Stress

This ancient form of Indian meditation focuses on the deep interconnection between mind and body. For 10 days, you are required to sit in silence and focus deeply on the physical and psychological sensations of the body – focusing the mind, moving through the various experiences with detached awareness.

The entire time you are at the retreat, you have no communication with the outside world, no interaction with the others in the retreat, and all of your senses are tuned in. For 10 days, it's all 'you' and it's all on! The day kicks off with a 4:00 am wake-up call, ready for 4:30 am meditation in the hall. You stop only to eat and sleep. The day ends at 9:30 pm, when you head back to your room, exhausted from a day inside your head! The whole Vipassana experience is for another book, but I wanted to write about my experience in this section of *Only Human* to articulate how much I learned about myself and about stress.

Throughout the retreat, my mind danced from one thought to the other, often frenetic, dramatic and disturbed. Thoughts about the physical pain I was experiencing (sitting down on the floor unsupported whilst being encouraged not to move for 10 hours is excruciating!), about the past, things I had done that I wasn't proud of, the people I had hurt, the people who had hurt me. Memories from decades ago came flooding back, and the faces of people I had long since lost touch with came to mind as the hours went by. Often, thoughts about what was happening at home popped into my head. One evening, the rain was coming down hard outside and I knew that my son Jack was going to watch the All Blacks play in our neighbouring city, Hamilton. To get there, you must drive through a hilly, dangerous stretch of road, notorious for its accidents. As the rain belted down on my small bedroom and the wind whipped across the trees and stream opposite, I felt a wave of dread. What if Jack was caught up in an accident on the way to the game? What if he's stuck in the car and can't get out? What if my husband couldn't get hold of me? All of these horrific thoughts flooded my system, and my maternal instincts were in overdrive as I tossed and turned, my mind playing sick games with me. In the middle of the night, I almost tapped out, ready to grab my things to leave and drive straight to the hospital! But something stopped me. It was day three. This was natural. It was normal. It was predictable. In the dark of night, sitting alone with no one to run to for help, I realised there were two storms that night. The one smashing around outside, but more importantly, the one that I had to wait and let pass in my mind.

That evening was pivotal for me because I realised the stress that is around me doesn't come from outside. It was all in my head. One thought had created a hurricane of negative and irrational emotions and none of it was based on facts. As the days passed, I settled into my new norm. Every time a similar dramatic thought entered my head, I would smile and compassionately bring myself back to the breath. Those ten days taught me so much about my habitual response and attachment to my thoughts. It taught me how to let go of the drama and to detach my expectation of the outcome in any given circumstance.

I still have a long way to go to become enlightened, but in the time that's passed since my first retreat, I have noticed that I am much less reactive to the external.

I am calmer, more focused and I can 'unhook' from the drama I have created in my head so much more easily. From my years in the fitness industry, I already knew the value of good sleep, nutrition and exercise, but this experience elevated that belief, showing how our tolerance to stress dramatically decreases if we aren't looking after the basics.

# Stress

When our stress response is triggered, we automatically respond by fight, flight, freeze or fawn. In a podcast I listened to recently, All Black Dan Carter talks about how you can see three of these instinctive responses (fight, flight, freeze) play out when the All Blacks faced France in the quarterfinals of the 2007 World Cup. As the favourites to win, France came from 13-0 down and won by just two points. Carter describes how the All Blacks caved under the pressure. Some, he said, showed their stress by arguing with the ref and getting aggressive with their opposition – fighting. Others developed cramps or got hurt, and just wanted to get out of there – flight. The rest looked around, stunned, not sure what to do next – freeze.

This is a perfect example of how we unconsciously react under pressure. Once we know how we most commonly react, we can work daily to build our tolerance, so that we save our stress response for emergencies, and not when we have forgotten to take the bins out on a rainy day.

The fourth, lesser talked about stress response is fawn. This is where someone, to reduce the risk of harm, will attempt to please the other person. I see this sometimes in coaching. My client might say something like, 'I don't want to say anything because I know it will start a row.' If this response isn't addressed, it can often lead to the person feeling like they have no say in a relationship, and they often find it difficult to set and stick to boundaries.

So, why do you react in the way that you do?

Whilst some people are genetically predisposed to higher stress levels than others, our conditioning also plays a big part in how we cope. The paternal side of my family are traditionally highly sensitive, empathetic, passionate and loving. The dark side to those qualities has resulted in overreaction, pain, anxiety, depression and addiction. When we are reunited for family functions, the physical family resemblance is uncanny, and when we catch up and swap stories, the 'It's the Pilgrim in us' line comes out! There's no hiding the fact that our genes are both a curse and a blessing.

Genes, though, are not to be used as an excuse. This tale perfectly sums it up:

> *There's an old story about two boys who had an alcoholic father. Those boys grew into young men.*
>
> *One son became an alcoholic too. 'What choice do I have?' he said. 'My father is an alcoholic.'*
>
> *The other son never touched a drop of alcohol. 'How could I?' he said. 'Look what it did to my father.'*

Whilst genes play a part, stress and how we respond to it again comes down to three things: mindset, awareness, choice.

Letting go of stress is easier said than done though. I understand that. Our circumstances and environment also play a huge role in our wellbeing. Some of the common stressors in life, such as finances and work, are based on security – our very primitive, instinctive need to feel safe.

Relationships, health, race, sex and gender inequalities are all factors and there's no denying the hard work that is required to pull ourselves out of the stress cycle.

## What does stress look like to you?

When the subject of stress comes up with my clients, some of them swear they don't feel stressed, yet their behaviour tells a different story. It doesn't always show up as anger and frustration. Like them, if you ever experienced:

- Reliance on alcohol, cigarettes, or drugs to relax
- Change in eating habits (eating more or less than usual)
- Putting off important jobs or projects
- Fear of failure
- Shallow breathing
- High or unrealistic expectations
- Perfectionism and comparison
- Increased time on screens
- Withdrawing from people and activities you enjoy

Chances are, you're in a stressed state.

## What can we do about it?

The theme running through *Only Human* is awareness. Awareness is the first step for change to happen. Becoming present or grounded gives us the space for us to think differently and choose a different ending.

A few years ago, my daughter and I were at loggerheads. We got caught in a negative loop resulting in below-the-line behaviours. We would regularly fight and say things we didn't mean. As the adult, I should have known better, but the reptile part of my brain, the amygdala, was ready to strike and this, unfortunately, stopped me from behaving rationally in the situation.

As time passed, I realised that our constant bickering (which always ended up in apologies, a kiss and a cuddle, by the way!) was wearing our family down. I was often distracted after a row and layered the situation with guilt. I blamed myself for not being able to be a 'better parent' and worried that I was damaging her in some way, which in turn reinforced my negative behaviour, so the cycle continued. Remember earlier, we talked about being careful what we look for? In this example, I was caught in the negative loop and could only see what was wrong in our relationship.

After some time and good chats with family and friends, I knew it was up to me to guide us out of the hole we were digging for ourselves. I decided to monitor every interaction I had with her and take 100 per cent responsibility for the way I responded to it.

The results were phenomenal.

Remember the sweet spot between stimulus and response? Well, this is the perfect place to add a mantra (a phrase to repeat to oneself), to encourage change. My mantra for this example was: 'There is another way.'

Every time I interacted with my daughter, Sienna, and I felt myself getting triggered (awareness), I stopped (grounded), and silently said, 'There's another way' (mantra).

This micro-moment empowered me to respond in a different way, which magically changed the energy and outcome. Instead of assuming she was having a go at me, I was fully present with her wants and needs. Most of the time, it turned out we both wanted the same things out of our relationship together, we just had different ways of displaying it.

Whilst Sienna and I still have our 'moments', they are now few and far between, and usually occur only when one or both of us haven't looked after our basic needs (sleep, good nutrition, exercise and a good dose of connection)

The power of this example is that it only took one person to change the outcome. We don't need to waste precious energy trying to change other people or situations, just our response to them.

On the back of my experience with Sienna, I created an acronym that I use for clients so they can apply it to stressful areas in their lives.

| A | = | Awareness |
|---|---|---|
| G | = | Grounding/being present |
| M | = | Mantra (positive, strong, intentional sentence) |

It's a game-changer for them, and I wonder if it might be for you.

## Resilience

Whilst each of us deals with stress differently, resilience is a skill that prepares us against the inevitable suffering that life throws at us.

One thing's for sure, building resilience helps people adapt better to life's curveballs, keeps self-esteem and confidence intact, allows people to handle setbacks without falling into victim and blame mentality and promotes a growth mindset that encourages us to look at life with curiosity and compassion rather than fear and judgement.

Resilience isn't about 'sucking it up' or taking an 'it is what it is' attitude to the stressors of life, more a quality that empowers us to step back, take a bird's eye view of a situation and compassionately process, accept and adapt to the challenges in front of us.

When looking at resilience through the lens of mindfulness, it becomes less about mental toughness and more about surrender. Having the courage to see the reality in front of us and dial into the thoughts, feelings and emotions that lie beneath, then moving forward with acceptance and understanding.

Resilience asks us to accept difficulty with courage. To work with it, not against it.

So, how can we build resilience and prepare for adversity?

### Increase self-awareness and invite curiosity

By understanding your habitual thought patterns, you will become more equipped to step out of default reactive behaviour when triggered by stress. You could start by asking yourself these questions:

- How do I currently react to triggering situations?
- What and who are my 'Achilles heels' in terms of triggering a stress response?
- What habitual responses do I currently have which aren't helpful?
- How does my body respond to stress?
- What tools do I already have to cope?

Being curious about how you react to situations will enable you to learn and grow rather than beat yourself up for responding in a certain way.

## Lean towards your emotions

Suppressing emotions long term undermines our resilience so it's important to get comfortable with noticing your emotions, recognising and labelling them.

- Do you push your emotions down or do you go over and over the same scenario, keeping you stuck in the same circumstance?
- Can you name the emotion you are feeling?
- What is causing the emotion?
- What would happen if you sat with the emotion and let it surface?

## Practise courage daily whilst living to your playbook of life

Knowing your values and living your life according to those values whilst challenging yourself daily to choose 'hard over easy' creates a compound effect when building resilience.

## Challenge yourself physically

The body and mind are intrinsically linked so it is vital to check in daily with your physical body. To protect your health, ensure you consult a physicisan before commencing any new regime.

- Find ways you can challenge yourself physically. Start jogging, play social sports, join a gym or learn that new hobby that's been on your mind.

- Implement a daily breath work or meditation practice.

- Introduce cold showers/cold water therapy to your morning routine.

Like anything worth learning, developing resilience will take consistency, commitment and vulnerability. Meeting yourself where you are at and boldly working through challenges with an open mind will develop an inner strength you didn't know you had.

## Have the power to forgive

Unless you have been living in a cave, chances are someone has hurt you. Someone from school. An ex. Your parents. Your boss. Your kids. Your partner. Yourself.

Being meaning-making machines, we hold on to the hurt and pain of other people's actions for far too long. Too many people have gone to their grave holding on to unresolved trauma and resentment, which could have been rectified.

When we are hurt by someone we trust and love, it can be very difficult to forgive them for their wrongdoings. The problem is that it can cause resentment, bitterness and mistrust in your current reality, which creates stress and reduces your chances of being happy.

Forgiveness to many looks like defeat, but to me it spells acceptance. It demonstrates compassion. It shows self-respect and willingness to move forward in your life without holding the negative emotions around you.

## Stress

Understanding the value of forgiveness will help you move through it and, just like the grieving process, it takes patience, time and courage to sit with the emotions that have most likely been suppressed because of what happened.

By holding on to negative past experiences, we become a victim of our past. Because of how our brain is wired, every time we remember a painful experience, our body responds with the same intensity as if it were happening in real-time. By harbouring resentment and pain for an experience that happened, you are loading your body with stress, reliving the hurt and pain.

To prove a point, let's do a little experiment together.

> Take a few big, deep breaths in and out, and when you are ready, lower and soften your gaze, continuing to breathe deeply and slowly. Imagine now that you are standing in your kitchen or the kitchen of someone you know.
>
> Now, bring your gaze to the counter and notice that there is a beautiful wooden cutting board there. On top of the board sits a bright yellow lemon. You notice its colour – a vibrant yellow – its size and shape.
>
> You reach out and pick up the lemon, noticing how it feels to your touch. The skin is both smooth and slightly bumpy; you may see the end where it was attached to the tree.
>
> Next to the cutting board, you see a sharp kitchen knife. Return the lemon to the cutting board and carefully pick up the knife in your dominant hand. Holding the lemon steady with your other hand, cut the lemon in half.

As you do this, you're feeling the knife slicing through the fruit and it falls open, revealing beautiful, jewel-like pulp in neat rows. You see the fresh white pulp and perhaps some seeds inside.

Drops of juice have spilled onto the cutting board. Now take one half of the lemon and cut it again, making a quarter-size slice.

Put the knife down and bring the lemon quarter up to your nose. Be aware of the sharp, fresh citrus scent filling your nose. Touch the lemon to your lips, noticing the sensations. Now, open your mouth and bite into the lemon.

What did you notice about the physical sensations when you were doing this? More than likely, your mouth started watering and perhaps when you went to take a bite you tasted the bitterness and winced a little?

This simple exercise demonstrates the strong relationship between our mind and body and how, using imagination alone, we have the power to transport ourselves. Just as when you're describing a fun, exciting moment to a friend, your body language is open and alive. When you relive a stressful, heart-breaking moment, your cells react as if in real-time.

Relating this to forgiveness, can you see how detrimental harbouring resentment and ill-will towards someone else does you more harm than good? How then can you move through the pain and towards freedom?

- Meditate – Taking the time to sit with the uncomfortable thoughts and feelings that arise will allow you to move through the painful moments more quickly.

- Acknowledge the pain they have caused you, using descriptive words. Be as specific as possible.

- Acceptance – Accepting harm inflicted on you or someone you love can be very difficult and confronting and may seem like you're letting them get away with it. On the contrary, by accepting what happened, you are freeing yourself of the pain of reliving the situation repeatedly.

- Connect with your values and journal the following questions:

How will forgiving _____
_____ give me peace?

What would my life look like if I were to let go of this resentment?

_____

_____

_____

_____

_____

**How would my life be different if I wasn't carrying this feeling?**

_____

_____

_____

_____

**What would my interactions with others be like?**

_____

_____

_____

_____

**How will forgiving a certain person move me towards living my values?**

_____

_____

_____

_____

In some cases, you might want to use talk therapy, such as counselling, or, if you are open to energy healing, powerful healing can occur with the right practitioner.

## What's weighing you down?

I was 14 when I decided I wanted to go travelling in Australia. I spent the next four years planning the trip, visualising my route, the people I would meet, the beaches I'd visit and the stories I'd have to tell upon my return.

It was all I could talk about. Australia was the country for me. It was back in the nineties so no mobile phones or internet. Just a copy of *Lonely Planet's Guide to Australia* and my imagination.

In the four years of preparation, I didn't think too much about what I was going to pack, so when the fateful day came, 26th October 1996, I said a tearful goodbye to my family and friends and left with a very heavy backpack, full of what I thought were very important things. Here's a handful of essentials I took:

- One pair of white jeans
- Two heavy 100 per cent cotton towels
- A large snowboarding woolly hat
- Some teddies
- Letters and cards my family and friends had written
- Photo album with photos of my friends and family

Now, as trendy as white jeans were back in the nineties, they were impractical things to pack on a six-month tour around Ozzy. The towels took up much-needed space and proved to be heavy when I got them wet. The woolly hat might have reminded me of my brother, but there wasn't much use for it in Perth's 35-degree heat. The teddies, letters and photos again provided some comfort when I was homesick (there was no Snapchat) but weighed me down considerably!

The long and short of it was: These 'essential' items wore me down when I was travelling from state to state, and there was no room for the important stuff and certainly no room for me to add more.

This story reminds me a little bit of life. We tend to fill our backpacks up with all the stuff we think we need (all the shoulds, needs and have-tos) and leaves us very little space for the stuff that matters: family, friends, purpose, joy, health.

On the following pages are three backpacks.

The first backpack represents the responsibilities and the energy thieves that are weighing you down and not serving you. The shoulds, the need-tos, the have-tos. In this first image, write down all the things that are stopping you from living life to the max – from the little things to the big things.

The second represents all the emotional baggage you are carrying. Some of it might not even be yours. For decades I carried around the burden of not having enough money, a bad habit I picked up from my dad. It wasn't until recently that I realised that HIS beliefs were stopping me from feeling safe when it came to money. Since I let it go, my relationship with money has changed and I have freed up mental energy for other things. Maybe it's the emotional baggage of someone else that you're carrying. Your partner's, children's, friends or co-workers' stress and bad mood perhaps.

## Stress

The final backpack, the Osprey of all packs, represents the life you want and deserve. Write down the actions and areas in your life that will give you energy, that will help you make the very most of your life, so you go to your grave with no regrets.

The items in this backpack mean something. They are worth the weight. What you put in here has meaning. It has grit. It is worth the pain.

Now, take a photo of your last backpack (or if you're using the *Only Human* companion workbook, print it off) and put it somewhere you can see it. Your fridge, bathroom mirror, the ceiling in your bedroom, in your car, anywhere that serves as a reminder that YOU GET TO CHOOSE what you carry around with you.

Just for the record, if I were to go back in time, I'd still take my photo album.

Only Human

AREAS OF MY LIFE THAT ARE WEIGHING ME DOWN

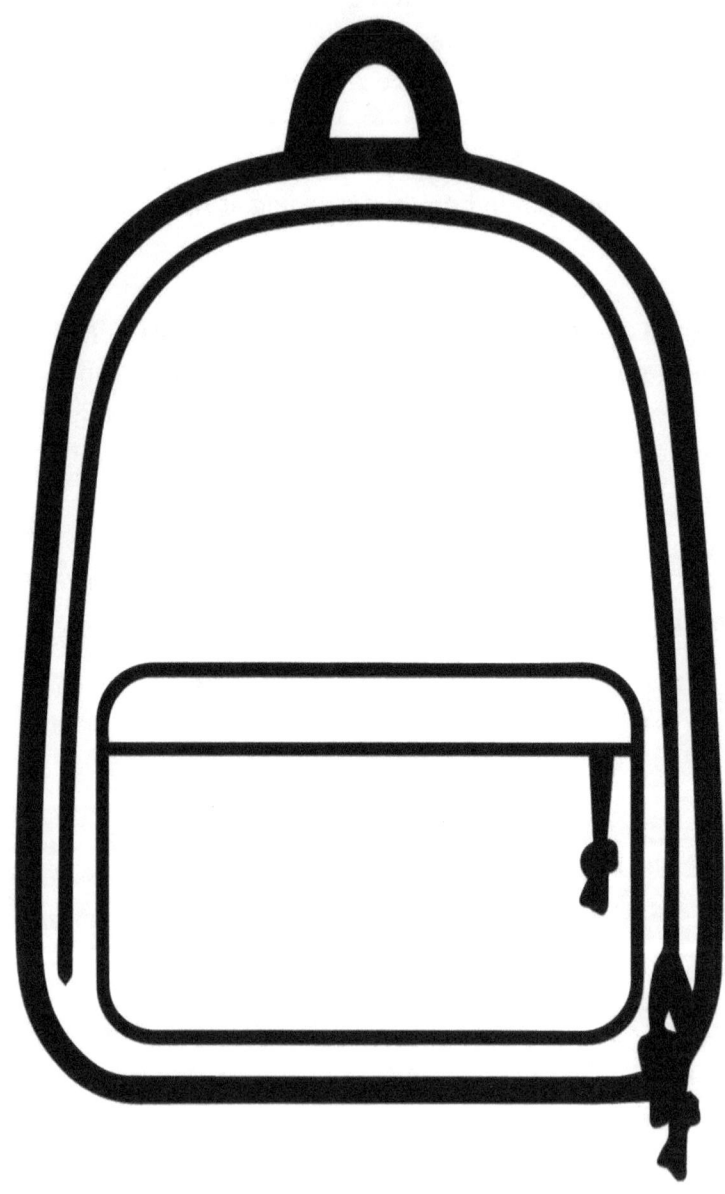

# Stress

**OTHER PEOPLE'S EMOTIONAL BAGGAGE I AM CARRYING**

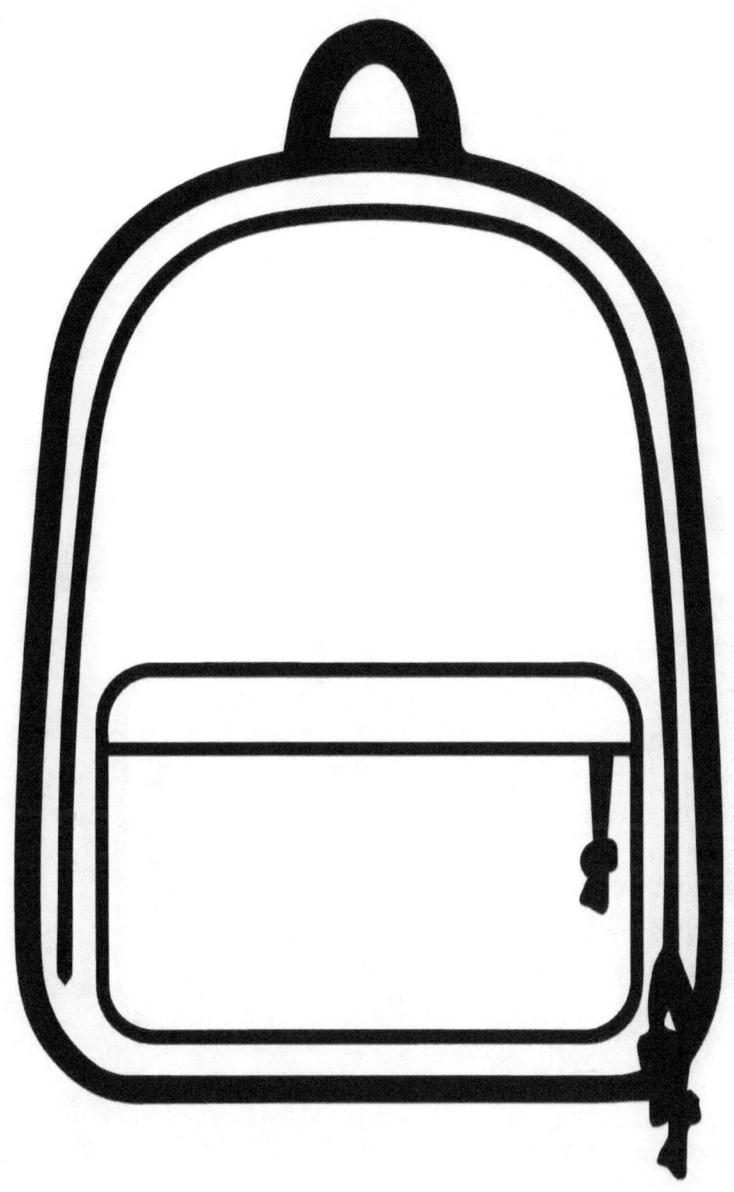

## Only Human

**THE LIFE I WANT AND DESERVE – MY BACKPACK ESSENTIALS**

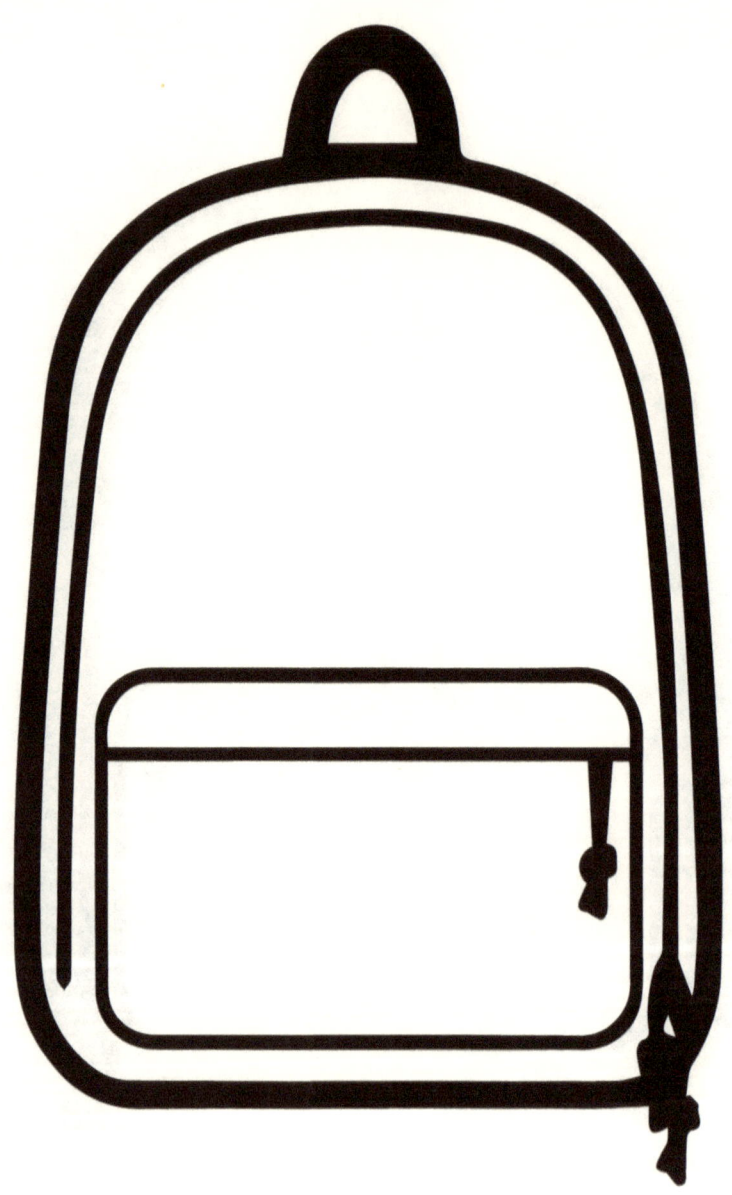

## Breathwork – it's (not) all in your head

I wish I knew then what I know now about breathwork. Maybe I might have been able to help Dad in his last few years of life. In his last decade, he suffered from debilitating arthritis, a heart complaint and other medical conditions. The list of medications he was prescribed gave him an even longer list of side effects, which reduced the quality of his life.

One of the severe side effects to his heart medication was shortness of breath. Always active, it frustrated him that short walks left him gasping for air and, over time, it wore him down. In his early years, he suffered TB, and consequently had acute surgery to the spine, leaving him with severe kyphosis (exaggerated rounding of the back), major scarring and altered posture. This alone restricted his ability to breathe well. It caused him to be immobile around the rib cage, reducing the strength of his diaphragm – a major respiratory muscle – and limiting his breath.

The muscles in his neck became hypertonic from overuse and he experienced constant pain in his jaw. The discomfort he felt day in, day out, along with the shortness of breath, became tiresome and, before long, he lost his appetite for life.

Although I wouldn't have been able to cure his symptoms, teaching him some basic breathing techniques would have dramatically improved his constitution.

Like most of us, his breathing wasn't efficient. It was shallow, as he breathed through his mouth, causing the muscles around his chest, neck and upper back to work harder than they needed to. His body adapted and this became his new baseline, which was poor.

## Only Human

Dad's poor breathing patterns accelerated his ill health.

When we are stressed, our breathing becomes irregular, shallow and it quickens, reinforcing the fight or flight response. Our breath becomes shallow, rapid and restrictive. If we can slow our breath down, our wellbeing will be enhanced.

Breathing is our life force, and spending time focusing on the breath can be deeply restorative.

This approach to stress works well for many, especially over-thinkers, for the fact that we move away from the thinking brain and into our deeply intelligent, internal system, accessing our innate wisdom and dialling into instinct. Often, through the work of breathing and meditation, stress and anxiety move through the body without the need for deep enquiry.

Ayurveda (which you will learn about later) and yoga use breathing exercises to reach optimal health and restore mental, spiritual and physical homeostasis. For most of us, breathing is something we take for granted, but if we pay attention to it, our lives could change in many positive ways.

The fight or flight response is activated by our sympathetic nervous system. Pranayama, or breathwork, helps activate the opposing system, the parasympathetic nervous system which aids the rest and digest pathways.

I use three simple breathwork exercises when I'm working with clients, all of which are game-changing. They literally change our body's physiology creating a different reaction to the external stimulus, resulting in fewer arguments, less resentment and reduced negativity.

Stress

The breathing exercises below can have strong physiological effects. Perform them in a safe place whilst sitting or lying down. Do not practise these techniques whilst driving, being in or around water or in other circumstances where you could cause yourself harm.

Audio versions can be found in your free bonus section.

## Diaphragmatic breathing

Benefits:

- Strengthens diaphragm
- Encourages relaxation
- Reduces heart rate
- Reduces blood pressure
- Takes strain off the muscles in the neck and jaw from poor habitual breathing techniques

How to:

- Sit down with a straight back or lie down on your back with your head supported (lying down is the easiest way to connect to the breath when you are a beginner)
- Place one hand on your tummy, just below your ribcage, and the other on your chest
- Close your eyes or keep a soft gaze
- Breathe in slowly through the nose, feeling your belly rise against your hand
- Keep your chest as still as you can
- Tighten the muscles in your tummy as you breathe out, pushing the air out of the lungs
- Repeat 5-10 times

## Box breathing

Benefits:

- Helps when you feel overwhelmed
- Slows down the mind
- Slows the heart rate
- Calms the nervous system
- Brings focus

How to:

- Sit up straight or lie down on your back with your head supported
- Close your eyes or keep a soft gaze
- Breathe naturally for a few breaths, focusing your attention on your diaphragm moving up and down, out to the sides and back
- Visualise a box of equal length
- Breathe in through the nose for the count of 4
- Hold your breath for the count of 4
- Breathe out through the nose for the count of 4
- Hold your breath for the count of 4

Repeat until you feel calm, alert and centred.

## Nadi Shodhana, alternating nostril breathing

Benefits:

- Balances the nervous system
- Improves breathing
- Balances the left and right sides of the brain
- Brings focus and calm

How to:

- Sit upright
- Bring your right hand up to your nose and move your forefinger and middle finger out of the way. Place your thumb on your right nostril
- With this nostril covered, close your eyes and exhale fully and slowly through your left nostril
- Exhale completely, release your right nostril and put your ring finger on the left nostril
- Breathe in deeply and slowly from the right side
- The breath is slow and continuous
- Once you've inhaled completely, exhale through your right nostril
- Release your ring finger and close your right nostril with your thumb again. Breathe in fully and exhale fully from your left nostril
- Repeat the full process for up to 10 minutes

## SUMMARY AND ACTIONS

- Breathwork is a powerful tool to shift out of overthinking, being overwhelmed, anxiety and habitual responses to life.

- A daily breathwork routine might seem just another thing to add to your busy life, but even committing to a couple of rounds of box breathing each day can have a positive impact.

- Breathwork is free, easy and life-enhancing.

- Choose and commit to one breathwork sequence for two weeks and log the difference in your mental and physical wellbeing.

- Take 100 per cent responsibility for your life. Catch yourself when you find yourself in a blame, judgement or victim mindset. Ask yourself if it's a helpful state to be in.

- Recognise that you can't change the external, but that you do have the ability to shift your perspective.

- Control the controllable. People spend a lot of energy and time worrying about things they can't control, whether that's other people's opinions, the weather, the past or other people's wellbeing.

- Dial in and focus on your own mindset by looking after your physical and mental wellbeing and how you treat others.

- Work on your mindset daily by completing the journaling and breathwork prompts in this book.

- Consider introducing a meditation practice.

- Prioritise the basics – physical exercise, nutrition and sleep.

- Connect with your values regularly.

- Where possible, remove the areas in your life that cause you stress.

- Unhook yourself from drama cycles.

- Practice increasing your physical and emotional tolerance to stress by pushing yourself, with compassion, out of your comfort zone.

- Forgive yourself and others for any wrongdoings so you can create space in your life for the good stuff!

The bottom line is that the mind is powerful, and it's within your grasp to harness that power. Take responsibility to create the right environment for your mind to thrive. Don't take the basics of health for granted. Check in with yourself often. Surround yourself with great people. Challenge yourself, your thoughts and beliefs. Be curious. Expand. Lean towards challenges with an openness to learn and grow. This incredible mind of yours is ready. The question is 'are you?'

When the body is strong, balanced and fit, our mental constitution can't help but positively change.

# 7

# Exercise

Humans were born to move. If you want to elevate your life, then you're going to have to push exercise up the order of your priorities.

Often kicked to the kerb with lack of time to blame, exercise can improve productivity, boost energy, increase creativity, lower stress and enhance concentration.

When the body is strong, balanced and fit, our mental constitution can't help but positively change. So, why, with all these benefits, does exercise get pushed to the bottom of the pile when life gets busy?

As we have mentioned, time, or the lack of it, in my experience, seems to be the biggest factor. Injury and the good old ego also feature heavily on the list of excuses not to train.

This chapter is dedicated to getting your edge back so you can enjoy the freedom that comes with feeling fit.

If exercise already features in your life and you're comfortable with how your progress is tracking, you might like to skim through this section and pick out the information that's relevant to you.

If you're like the hundreds of other busy people looking at your diary, wondering where on earth you're going to find the time, trust me and read on. We can find time together.

Time is an interesting phenomenon. We rule our lives by it and yet it seems to have an agenda of its own. How come some days feel like an eternity, and yet others fly by? A second is a second. A minute is a minute. Therefore, time, we could argue, is irrelevant.

Talking again from my own experience and that of others, time isn't the problem. It's our perception of time and our expectation to be able to do everything in equal measure. This comes from our all-or-nothing thinking that I have been guilty of many times in my life. All-or-nothing thinking can land us in a lot of trouble when it comes to finding the time.

Let's take exercise as our example, because we are In the nutrition chapter, and feel free to use it in other areas of your life where you might be limiting yourself.

I was working with someone recently who knew that exercising was going to make him feel better. He listed off all the benefits he would experience. Some, no doubt, would be like your list. 'I'd have more energy, I'd look better, I'd feel better, I'd be able to keep up with my kids' sports, I'd feel more confident with my partner and my back wouldn't hurt as much.'

## Exercise

When I asked him what he was going to do, he said he was going to run four times per week and try to fit in one or two of the on-demand Pilates classes I teach as well.

Whilst his intentions were great, this was a guy who hadn't made time for himself in a couple of years and was flat out with work and parenting duties. This hardcore personality was at risk of burning out during the first week of training.

We talked about the reality of his situation and how important it was to introduce new habits slowly. To make them so easy that he couldn't possibly fail. Being of the all-or-nothing nature myself, I found it hard to offer this as a suggestion, but knew from experience if we didn't start slowly, that he wouldn't achieve his long-term goal – to be fit, strong and injury-free for his 40th birthday.

Instead of loading him with unrealistic, weekly tasks, we started with two weeks of setting the alarm 10 minutes earlier than usual and getting up to do 10 minutes of stretching. He also committed to taking his allocated lunch break instead of eating at his desk. We then built up his incremental fitness.

These two small changes were a big step forward to his starting and, more importantly, continuing an exercise regime. The key was to start small, making it easy to do. Remember the feel-good hormone I mentioned in the gratitude section of the book? This is where it gets released again. The reward system in the brain kicked in, as a flood of happy hormones entered his system, reinforcing the experience as a good one. One to repeat. And repeat he did. As the weeks passed and the new habit was formed, we increased the length of time he trained, by adding a short walk, which soon became a jog, which then became his weekly unmissable routine.

To this day, he still puts his exercise routine first. Because of the slow and steady approach, instead of 'go hard or go home', he was able to build exercise into a consistent, habitual routine.

Habits are a big topic and the master on the subject, James Clear, talks in depth about how to build sustainable, healthy habits in his book, *Atomic Habits*. Essentially, building new habits takes time. They are unconscious and fly under the radar, designed by the brain to save time. That's why it's so easy to be confronted by how many empty beers and wine bottles are in the recycling when you only perceive you've had one or two to relax. Creating new habits feels like an effort at the start because it is! You must consciously take new actions repetitively and consistently, to rewire the brain until it becomes 'normal'.

If you have been around children who learn how to tie their shoelaces, you will notice how much time, patience and repetition are required for them to grasp the concept. It can be painfully frustrating for the person teaching them, but to the child, it takes energy, concentration and persistence! It's the very same for us when we look to introduce a new regime, hence it is vital to make it EASY. So easy, you can't fail.

The focus of building a healthy lifestyle routine is to create a habit, which, once established, takes more effort NOT to do than do!

So, what can you do in your own life that will make moving so easy that you can't fail?

## Exercise

Take some time to write down some ideas now:

(e.g. Prepare exercise clothes the night before, get a walking buddy, hire a personal trainer, 10 press-ups before I have my breakfast, walk up the stairs instead of taking the escalator.)

_____

_____

_____

_____

**HABIT:**
A settled or regular tendency or practice, especially one that is hard to give up.

**AUTOPILOT:**
Doing something without thinking about it, or without trying.

**A few words on motivation**

You can't rely on it!

So many of us rely on feeling motivated before we start a project or wellness journey. You might have experienced it yourself. You join a gym challenge, get yourself in the zone, inspired by all the before and after shots of previous winners, (It always makes me giggle seeing how tanned the bodies are in the after photos!), you head to the health food shop for your quinoa and kale. Motivation is high, an alarm is set for 4:30 am, Monday, and you're out of bed and into it by 5:00 am. You maintain your motivation for a week, maybe even two. With the lack of calories in your salad and smoothie, an aching body and no change on the scales, despite your efforts slowly wearing you down, by the third week, your motivation has slipped. You start pressing snooze, slipping a cheeky flat white back into your morning and by week four, you've tapped out.

Motivation is fleeting and has no staying power. It also leads you down the go-hard or go-home track, which doesn't bode well for long-term change.

In contrast, plenty of us stay stuck in our comfort zone, waiting to feel motivated before we take the first step. In my experience, people spend years waiting to feel like it, only to say, 'I wish I had done that when I was younger.'

**Don't wait until you feel like it**

The message here is to put feelings aside and develop a mechanism to support your exercise regime and relate feelings to your values.

One of my core values is connection. I love having meaningful conversations, laughing until my belly hurts, helping others and feeling connected to the people I'm around. Personally, when I don't exercise, my confidence drops. When I'm not feeling fit, I'm less engaged with the world. So, it's important to me to exercise so it brings me closer to my value of connection. By moving my body daily, I increase the likelihood of connecting with those around

## Exercise

me. There are days when I don't feel like training, but because I have disciplined myself to act regardless of how I feel, I still put the effort in and, naturally, feel better as a result.

The reality is, in the beginning, it is unlikely that you are going to feel like training. Building in systems and linking the benefits of you exercising to your values are going to be the keys to your success.

> Now it's your turn. Thinking back to your core values, take time to write about how exercise will directly tap into what matters the most.
>
> How will being fit, healthy and strong bring me more of what I desire in life?
>
> _____
>
> _____
>
> _____
>
> _____
>
> What systems will I build into my day to ensure I succeed?
>
> _____
>
> _____
>
> _____

## 'The future depends on what we do in the present.' – Mahatma Gandhi

The reality is that tomorrow is your today. Creating a solid discipline will secure your roadmap toward living a healthy lifestyle. Within a matter of months, new habits will be formed and it will feel odd if you don't exercise.

### What exercise should I do?

When it comes to exercise, there is something for everyone. Like nutrition, which we will address in the next chapter, it can be confusing and overwhelming when trying to decide where to start, so let's begin with what you enjoy.

For some, it's the feeling of being outside in nature – perhaps outdoor swimming, surfing, walking, jogging or biking might hit the spot. For others, the social side of a sport like indoor cricket, football or touch rugby might be more inspiring. Maybe learning a new hobby like karate or jiu-jitsu appeals. Yoga and Pilates are fantastic modalities to strengthen the body and mind and are becoming more and more popular with sportsmen and women around the world. As for me, I love the gym. I love to hit a boxing bag, explore what my body can do from a strength perspective, and challenge myself. Me against me.

The opportunities to move the body are endless, so, really, it's a case of dialling into how you want to spend your time. There is, of course, the school of thought that we must do things we don't like to achieve our overall goal and, whilst I understand the concept, I do believe there is enough choice when it comes to exercise, to find something you like.

## Exercise

It's hard enough to find the time to train, let alone do an activity you hate! The bottom line is that moving your body is an essential part of the wellbeing puzzle. Without it, you can't expect to feel your best. Take this opportunity to brainstorm activities you would like to do and why.

**Exercise:** _____

Why I'd like to participate:

_____

_____

Local clubs near me that I can look to join:

_____

_____

Someone I could go with:

_____

_____

When I'll go and try it out:

_____

_____

**Exercise:** _____

Why I'd like to participate:

_____

_____

Local clubs near me that I can look to join:

_____

_____

_____

Someone I could go with:

_____

_____

_____

## Exercise

When I'll go and try it out:

_____

_____

**Exercise:** _____

Why I'd like to participate:

_____

_____

Local clubs near me that I can look to join:

_____

_____

Someone I could go with:

_____

_____

When I'll go and try it out:

_____

_____

_____

## How often should I exercise?

In an ideal world, you would move your body daily for up to 30 minutes to reap the positive health benefits, Consider mobility, strength, cardio, balance and flexibility components. When you begin more strenuous activity, ensure you build in a decent warm-up and cool-down. A few token stretches at the end might have been OK when you were in your teens, but it's a different story when we hit our mid-30s and above! It's worth bearing in mind, from a weight loss perspective, you can't beat good quality nutrition which we will cover later.

Non-exercise activity thermogenesis (NEAT) is the energy we expend when we aren't exercising, sleeping or eating. It's not often talked about, and it's not sexy, but moving our bodies when doing our daily tasks expends energy, which compounds over the course of a few months or a year. This can be great for fitness and weight loss. Too much emphasis, in my opinion, is spent on structured exercise to lose those extra kilos. From experience, it's the other 23 hours of the day that count.

You can be clever about how to increase the energy you expend by moving more incrementally. Use the stairs instead of the lift, park your car in the furthest part of the car park and walk, go to do the groceries instead of getting them delivered, walk when you are talking on the phone and use a standing desk. All those incremental steps will make a difference over the course of a year and will help you keep the unwanted weight off.

I love this way of moving as it weaves in mindfulness too. Chores can be arduous and get in the way of the things you want to do at the weekends, but if you reframe everyday jobs and see them as bonus points to burn fuel, mowing the lawns, taking the bins out and walking the dog when it's pouring down outside, they suddenly serve a bigger purpose!

Pay attention to your body so you can exercise beneficially. Some days your body can go hard, while other days you need something gentler and more restorative. If you're into tracking your fitness stats, there are plenty of options available to you, ranging from watches to rings, all giving valuable information that can enhance your performance.

Think back to the chapter on how your body responds to stress. Back in the day, we would have used the energy to fight or run, but our modern stressors mostly don't require us to do that, and this is where a good workout can come in. Just last week, I was feeling a bit tapped out off the back of a big week of writing and coaching. Except for walking and Pilates, I hadn't done much in the way of movement, and I could feel my mood was prickly. I've got a great personal trainer who, from a message I sent him, picked up my mood and told me to get my boxing gloves and come on over. We smashed out a session and it felt incredible. Instead of reacting negatively to the energy inside me, I was able to use exercise to move the energy through me and be a better human afterwards.

## Be careful not to overdo it

My time working at Saracens Rugby Club was a great learning experience for me in many ways. One thing that fascinated me was the players' work rate. Their ability to train hard during the week, perform at the highest level during the match at the weekend and then come back ready to go again. One of the reasons they were able to sustain such a high-intensity training load day in, day out, is because the coaching staff factored in rest. During one meeting before a big game, the coach told the boys to go home and do nothing. Not even wandering around the shops. Rest was imperative to their performance.

This is an extreme example of how the body needs to rest, but if you are suffering from chronic stress, haven't exercised in a while and go all in by depleting yourself of calories and embarking on extreme, high-intensity exercise, you will find yourself exhausted and more susceptible to sickness and injury.

It's a fine balance, and the more you tune in to your body, the more you will find the sweet spot that takes you into a positive routine. Establish a habit first. Make it too easy to miss and build up from there. In a matter of months, you will find yourself feeling fantastic.

## Find yourself a Roy

About a year into my personal training career, I met Roy. He was an ex-rugby pro and a machine. When I met with him to discuss his training requirements, he said he wanted me to push him hard in our sessions. After 10 gruelling weeks of boxing, running, rowing and calisthenics he had inspired me so much that I asked him if we could become training buddies. For the years that followed, I had never been fitter. He was 10 years my senior, so what I lacked in physical strength, being a woman, I made up for with my youth. We would pick each other up when we were down, and sense each other's mood, sometimes before the other one would. Some days, we left it all on the gym floor, but for others we knew to take it easier so we could rest and come back strong. We developed a friendship over sweat, dedication and commitment to each other. There were days when one of us couldn't be bothered, but we showed up anyway. During those years, I felt so supported and I know he did too. For

## Exercise

over a decade we trained together two to three times a week and still meet up now when I head back to my hometown in England.

If you can find a decent training buddy, your relationship to exercise will change, so do yourself a favour: find yourself a Roy.

Not convinced? Evidence suggests that when you train with someone else, you are far more likely to maintain consistency and discipline. You are also less likely to experience negative self-talk and self-sabotage. If you want to experience a higher work rate and create more accountability, then finding a training partner, especially in the early stages of establishing your exercise routine, is the way to go.

Training partners don't have to be friends. Roy and I didn't start that way. I had tried exercising with a couple of mates before, but it was too easy for excuses to creep in and for our sessions to become filled up with chat. Of course, if you can find a friend with the same goals as you and who is reliable – that's a bonus – but think outside the box when it comes to who you could share your exercise time with.

I held a workshop at a small business a couple of years ago and off the back of that they set up a lunchtime training session. They alternated running with circuit sessions after one of the team decided to bring her weights in for everyone to share. Amazing!

Post-COVID, a group of local dads decided they were going to play indoor cricket, so they set up a WhatsApp group and before they knew it, they had a team. Epic!

The thing with exercise is that most people want to do more, but most people don't take the time for it. So, if you can be the one to take the initiative to set something up, then you're doing others a favour too. Time with others AND movement! Happy days.

> Can you think of a handful of people you could ask to train with?
>
> Write a list here:
>
> _____
>
> _____
>
> Write the date by which you will have set up your first session:
>
> _____
>
> _____

## Get outside

Never have we spent so much time indoors. Our lives have become very insular, and even before COVID times, I met lots of people whose only time outside was going from their house into the car, and from the carpark into the office. Post-COVID, more people have the option to stay at home, making it even easier to skip a moment of fresh air.

More research is being done on the impacts of increased exposure to nature, forests, water and the elements. Not only does it help our resilience to the changing temperatures (rather than staying

Exercise

in our cosy comfort zone), but studies have shown that being in nature can lower blood pressure, improve mood and reduce the stress hormone, cortisol, in the body.

It's intuitive. Spend any time by the water and chances are you will immediately feel more relaxed. This is because powerful neurochemicals are transmitted through the body when we are in or around water. Perhaps, too, our innate wisdom understands that we are made up of 70 per cent water and on a biological level we connect, knowing that water symbolises life.

Whatever the reason, there's no denying that a dose of nature is good for the soul.

I would encourage you to get outside as much as you can, even if you live in an urban area. Find a park and take yourself there frequently. If you have a garden, make the effort to go outside barefoot, cloud gaze, star gaze, just 'be'. No phones, no distractions, just you and nature.

**Simple ways to connect with nature**

Walk barefoot in your garden.

Go for a walk without headphones.
Use four of your senses: sight, sound, touch, and smell to notice your surroundings.

Plan trips to the beach or the woods/bush.

Create a nature hub at home.
Herbs, pot plants and indoor plants.

Exercise outside
come rain or shine.

## SUMMARY AND ACTIONS:

- If you don't make time for exercise, your health will suffer.

- Building positive habits by making exercise easy to do will improve your chances of success.

- Exercising outside in nature will improve your mental and physical well being.

- Finding movement that you enjoy will increase the likelihood of you continuing.

- Don't wait until you feel like exercising. Build a routine into your schedule and go regardless of your feelings.

- All or nothing thinking is a trap. Start small and build up.

- Work through the journaling prompts in this section

- Find yourself a Roy.

If you believe that making time to eat gets in the way of other more important things like work and you want to transform your life, it's time to change the way you think.

# 8

# Nutrition

Influencers on social media would love for you to believe that nutrition is confusing, but the reality is that it's not that complicated. If you're eating too much of the wrong things, you will accumulate body fat, your skin will look dull, you will feel lethargic, snore when you sleep and wake up feeling sluggish. In the long term, you are at risk of developing unsavoury diseases like type II diabetes, heart disease, high blood pressure, autoimmune diseases and cancer.

There's no escaping the effects of a poor diet, and the modern Western diet is full of unhealthy, energy-depleting substances that increase the strain on our bodies rather than healing us.

Inflammation in the body, caused by poor diet, stress and dehydration can lead to weight gain, chronic fatigue, mental health problems, joint pain, irritable bowel syndrome and other gut issues.

If you want to look and feel good, have more energy and reach your potential, balanced nutrition must be high up on your list of priorities.

Out of all of the MENS components, nutrition is the one I struggle with the most. I am a long-time lover of tea and when I had the kids, I adopted a habit of drinking far too much of it in place of nutritious meals. So, as someone who likes to practise what I preach, and someone who values honesty, if nutrition is your stumbling block, then I'm right beside you.

I wrote earlier about controlling the controllable and how taking 100 per cent responsibility for your life is one of the biggest positive shifts in mindset you can have. When it comes to nutrition, once you change your mindset and use food for fuel and connection, you will accelerate your personal and spiritual growth.

If you believe that making time to eat gets in the way of other more important things like work and you want to transform your life, it's time to change the way you think.

When it comes to weight loss, it's a relatively easy problem to fix. If you're consuming more calories than you expend each day, you will put on weight. It's a simple calculation – energy in versus energy out. Educating yourself on how many calories you need each day will empower you to increase your movement and reduce your calorie intake to suit your weight loss requirements.

How many calories you need per day will depend on your age, lifestyle, weight loss goals and how much you exercise. Apps like MyFitnessPal provide tools to calculate your maximum daily calories for weight loss and maintenance, as well as accountability and motivation.

## Nutrition

When I was a personal trainer, I looked at my client's eating habits to see where they were sneaking in extra calories. If they had a cup of tea, did they have a biscuit with it? Did they add sugar to their hot drinks? What about sauces, ketchup and mayonnaise? When they had a big night out, they invariably ate 'crap' the next day. Remember, habits are unconscious. We can't see calories sneaking in if we don't become aware.

One of my clients swore blind that he didn't drink much, but the recycling bin outside his house, each week, told a different story. It wasn't until I highlighted this to him that he had the 'oh, right, I get it!' moment!

Over time, as my weight loss clients' awareness increased and they understood the choices they faced, it became easier for them to change their eating habits.

Spend some time over the next few days noticing where those extra calories you're eating are coming from.

What foods do I pick at mindlessly?

_____

_____

_____

_____

> What am I noticing about my eating habits that are helpful to my health goals?
>
> _____
>
> _____
>
> _____
>
> _____

To function optimally, our body needs a balance of water, carbohydrate, protein, fat, vitamins and minerals.

**Water.** It isn't the most exciting drink on the planet, but it does wonders for our health. As well as the usual suspects like yellow urine, headaches, dull skin and thirst as symptoms of dehydration, sugar cravings, embarrassingly bad breath and lack of energy can also appear.

The human body is made of up to 70 per cent water. It helps lubricate joints, helps deliver oxygen to the body, regulates our body temperature, flushes out waste from the body and much more. Water is essential to optimal performance. Water is essential for our survival.

Water is the ultimate super tonic, yet in my years coaching people, drinking more water has typically been met with a lot of resistance. Some people say it bloats them; others say they

## Nutrition

have to wee too much. Some don't like the taste and others don't believe the hype.

Alan, a client of mine, wasn't a water lover. He was a successful, hard-working, busy man looking for the extra edge. He was grateful for the lifestyle he had worked hard to build and wanted to have the energy to enjoy it.

When the subject of water came up, he dismissed it and told me about his preferred choices: coffee and energy drinks. Water was boring, underrated and off the cards.

I've never been one to tell clients what to do, as it doesn't work, and this case was no different. Casually, I asked him, 'How would your life change if you believed water gave you the energy you're looking for?' We moved on and talked about other things and the session ended. A couple of weeks later, Alan arrived for a catch-up with a bounce in his step, more than usual. When I asked him how he'd been, he revealed he'd started drinking a couple of bottles of water a day and he was shocked at the amount of energy he had gained. This energy made him focused, engaged and fun to be around. Water had helped him achieve his number one goal, 'To have energy for the things I love.'

If you, like many others, are sitting on the fence when it comes to water, how about trying an experiment for two weeks. Highlight any of these symptoms that you currently experience and commit to increasing your water intake, to 500ml bottle a day until you reach two litres.

Note down how you currently feel and then reassess in two weeks to compare the difference.

Signs that you might be dehydrated:

- Low energy
- Brain fog
- Bad breath
- Yellow urine
- Headaches
- Dull skin
- Thirst
- Constipation
- Muscle cramps

As well as drinking more water, you can also increase your water intake by eating seasonal fruits and green, leafy vegetables. The bonus is that it boosts your fibre intake which will also improve your digestion.

Eliminating or reducing your caffeine will allow your body to absorb the water you take on throughout the day.

Where possible, drink water at room temperature or slightly warmed. As much as cold water tastes good at the time, especially on a summer's day, the body has to work harder to reduce the temperature and takes longer to absorb.

Adding a pinch of good quality sea salt will save you money on energy drinks and offer you similar benefits. By adding salt to your water, you will fast-track your hydration and give the body essential minerals to support the body's needs, whilst avoiding the highly processed diabetes-inducing energy drinks.

# Nutrition

Water goals:

| Current daily water intake | Current daily caffeine/ energy drink/fizzy drinks/ cordial |
|---|---|
|  |  |
| Goal | How I will reach my intended water consumption goal |
|  |  |

## A word from Alan

*Having achieved all my business and personal goals by the age of 55, I sat on the couch one morning wondering whether I had lost the plot as I had never felt so underwhelmed in life. I felt unmotivated and disengaged with my surroundings. On the surface, I had everything in life, a successful business, strong marriage, close family, time and money.*

*Yet, I had forgotten to look after me. I had lost the guy I once was – an energetic, colourful, happy bloke who looked up to Chris Martin as a role model. I was grumpy and struggling with the fact that my teenagers were now adults living their own busy lives. I had lost my sense of purpose. I just needed to get this energetic, colourful lead singer from Coldplay back on stage again, but didn't know how! After a while, my wife suggested I have a casual chat to this cool chick, Anna, and, after catching up for a quick chat and a terrible cup of coffee, I enrolled in her eight-week coaching programme.*

*The sessions have enabled me to enjoy life once again. I have a new sense of direction, understanding how to do the basics well. Good food intake, drinking water and keeping on top of my physical and mental wellbeing.*

*To the cool chick who helped guide a grumpy old man back to Chris Martin again, thanks mate.*

*P.S. Water is good for you, even if it is colourless and boring!*

**Carbohydrates** have been demonised over the years but are an essential part of balanced nutrition. Carbohydrates, or carbs, are an important energy supply for our diet and can be found in most foods. The healthiest way of getting carbs into your body is by increasing your vegetable and fruit intake, eating wholegrain bread and cereal and brown rice and pasta.

**Protein** plays the important role of growing and repairing body tissue. Protein is a building block made up of amino acids that form healthy muscles, hair, skin and nails. We can use protein for energy when needed and whilst we can make some of our amino acids, we rely on food to give us the ones we can't produce. Foods high in protein include venison, chicken, beef*, lamb*, pork*, fish/seafood, quinoa, beans, lentils, chickpeas, tofu, mung beans, split peas, eggs, cheese, yoghurt, milk, chia seeds and protein powder.

\*These are high in saturated fat, so consume infrequently.

**Fat**, like its mate, carbohydrate, has been given a hard time over the years, but it is an essential component to optimal health. It helps to protect your vital organs, supports cell growth and assists the body in absorbing nutrients. Problems arise when we eat too much of the wrong fat, mostly found in baked and processed foods and red meat. Avocados, nuts, seeds and olive oil are wildly beneficial to your health. Including flaxseed oil, hemp seeds, coconut oil, sesame oil, tahini and LSA to your diet will supercharge your health.

**Vitamins and minerals** are essential for helping the body fight infection, regulate our hormones, increase bone density and increase healing time. We can become deficient in vitamins for many reasons, including inflammation in the body, gut issues, too much acidity in the body and hormonal imbalances.

Eating a well-balanced, varied diet should give you what your body needs. In some cases, though, additional support is required. Hormonal imbalance, insomnia, recovering from sickness, chronic stress or burnout are all examples of when supplements might help. The global supplement market sits at about $71.81 billion, so before you get drawn into the latest 'take this pill and you will feel great' marketing bait, I highly recommend investing in seeing a qualified nutritionist, Ayurveda practitioner or herbalist so they can recommend the right supplements for your constitution.

## Convenience food

With the pace of life at an all-time record-breaking sprint, convenience food is a short-term fix for hunger, but it creates health problems in the long run. Most convenience food is high in fat, sodium, sugar and synthetic substances made by scientists paid to find the hard-to-resist taste, so, to quote the old Pringles advert – 'Once you pop, you can't stop.'

Chemically processed foods include artificial substances, chemical flavouring and sweeteners, which our body doesn't recognise and can't utilise, but they taste good so our reward-seeking brain learns to want more of them despite their detrimental impacts.

Here are some foods that might give you instant gratification but are void of nutritional value are listed below.

- Sugary breakfast cereals (including 'healthy options' like granola, porridge with added flavourings and store-bought muesli)
- Crisps/chips and crackers
- Sweets
- Ice cream
- Baked goods
- Fried goods
- Instant noodles
- Fizzy drinks
- Energy drinks
- Reconstituted meats, including ham, salami, bacon, nuggets and sausages
- Protein bars
- Ready meals

If you're looking at the list and feeling overwhelmed because it's full of your favourite foods, you're not alone. In the Western world, we have been conditioned by major food corporations into believing that these foods make us happier. We have fallen into the trap of believing that it is quicker and easier to pick up these items, smash

## Nutrition

them down (let's face it, they taste great in the moment) and get on with something more important (being productive, working, getting on with the next thing)!

Author of the books, *Salt, Sugar, Fat and Hooked,* Michael Moss, explains that food companies have the power to manipulate their customers' eating habits by producing food high in sugar, fat and salt which excite the reward centre of the brain. The food companies are literally getting us hooked on these foods which are killing us slowly.

Everywhere we look, and even where we don't look (marketing companies use strategies to bypass the conscious mind and sell to our subconscious), the messages to eat these foods is out there and the food companies continue to make billions. The sad thing is, for many people looking to improve health and lose weight, they often feel like failures when they can't give up these foods. They perceive themselves to be weak, and lacking willpower, reinforcing the belief that they will never be able to change and it's all too hard.

If you are like the millions of others who rely on convenience and fast food, I want you to hear this. You are NOT weak. It is NOT about willpower.

Since you are now someone who takes 100 per cent responsibility, you can take this newfound awareness and CHOOSE a different response. Here's an example of how you can do this.

One of my bad habits is buying 'treats' from the petrol station. My favourites: a packet of salt and vinegar crisps and a bar of chocolate. I've been driving for 27 years. I buy petrol once a week, so that's roughly 1,408 opportunities for me to reinforce the habit of eating these foods.

Knowing the petrol station is a trigger for me, I have a rule now: to buy my petrol from the pump.

Most of the time this works, and I've noticed that when I'm tired, hungry or stressed, I'm more likely to think, 'stuff it' and go hard on the chocolate and crisps. This is just another example of how making MENS an absolute priority is pivotal for the success of our health.

Below is a modified diagram of the habit loop created by American journalist Charles Duhigg which shows us how to understand how habits work. I've used my example of the petrol station to illustrate the process our brain takes when we have a craving.

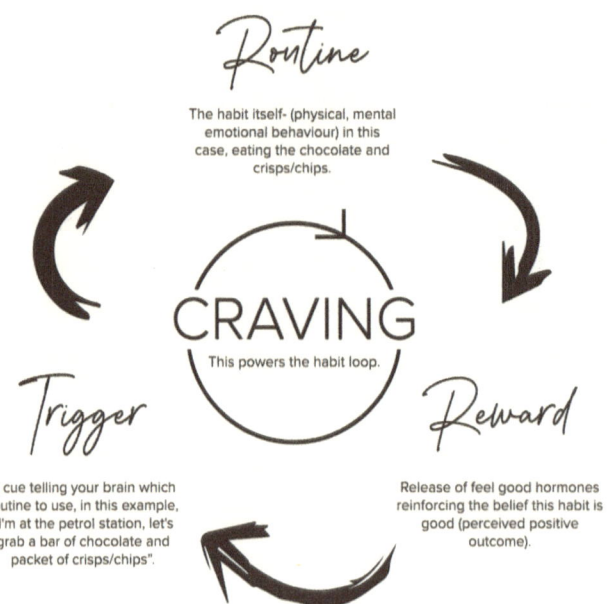

# Nutrition

**Now it's your turn. Use the habit loop to ascertain your routines when a craving strikes.**

_____

_____

_____

_____

_____

*Routine*
Insert your habit here:

**CRAVING**
This powers the habit loop.

*Trigger*
Insert your trigger here:

*Reward*
Release of feel good hormones reinforcing the belief this habit is good (perceived positive outcome).

## Building good habits

Our brain uses habits to create efficiency so when you decide to create new habits, it will take some time to make those changes stick. We like to do what we have always done so being patient and curious will help you achieve these changes.

Creating new habits takes time so set the right environment to succeed. Here's how to build a healthy habit and make it stick:

- Be clear on what you want to change.

- Link that goal to your values. Why is it important to you, and how will it be positive for you and those around you?

- Do the work to get to the cause of the habit. Is there anything you need to address – work stress, financial concerns, family turbulence, self-esteem?

- Understand your triggers and interrupt the loop.

- When the thought arises, sit with the thought, allow the craving to rise and pass. Use the QR code at the back of this book to listen to the craving meditation session.

- Reduce temptation by making it difficult to succeed in your old habit.

- Make your new habit too easy to fail.

- Call on friends and family to create accountability.

- To create new neural pathways, catch yourself in the habit loop.

## Nutrition

Now that you know a little bit about what our body needs and doesn't need in terms of fuel for optimal health, and you understand the brain's habit loop response, you will be able to identify some of your own triggers. Your aim now is to introduce as many good-quality food items slowly and intentionally into your diet, whilst reducing empty-calorie foods without feeling deprived.

Here are some ideas of 'rules' I've suggested to clients in the past that have worked a treat!

- Eat at the dinner table only – this cuts out the undesirable habits that are loaded with calories that you don't need
- Eat three times a day and drink water in-between
- Start with your biggest meal in the morning and reduce portion size at lunch, with your lightest meal at night, before 7:00 pm where possible
- Move tempting food out of sight
- Assess your hunger – are you hungry or using food as a distraction for another emotion? Boredom, anxiety, anger, etc
- Sit with the craving, let it rise and pass – what else might you be craving? (e.g. social connection, rest)

The consistent message throughout this book is to make changes easy and meaningful. To challenge the beliefs that are holding you in patterns that don't support your overall wellbeing so, in the end, it's less about deprivation and more about choice. That's 100 per cent responsibility right there!

From today, what will you stop, start and continue when it comes to your nutritional needs?

I will STOP _____

I will START_____

I will CONTINUE _____

So, what does this all mean to you? If, like Alan, you've lost a bit of your sparkle, then getting back to basics and doing them consistently well is your ticket to feeling like the best version of yourself again.

Zoom out and see the bigger picture. Commit to consistently putting high-quality, nutrient-dense fuel in your tank.

What nutrient-dense foods do you currently, consistently fuel your body with?

_____

_____

_____

_____

_____

What do you crave and feel attached to that gives you emotional comfort but might be holding you back from feeling your best?

_____

_____

_____

_____

## Caffeine

Seattle, with its evergreen forests, stunning coastal views and bold architecture, was the city where I learned my lesson about the negative effects of caffeine. I was 19 years old, and on my way home from my six-month tour of Australia, with my white jeans a dodgy shade of grey. My older brother, Mike, had set me up to stay with his model friend, Steve, who also owned a juice bar in Downtown Seattle. Being underage to drink, the only shot I experienced that trip was a wheatgrass shot with a fresh, clean taste that I still recall to this day.

For the next four days, Steve showed me around the city and made sure it made a lasting impression on my soul. One afternoon, he invited me to one of his modelling jobs. As I was underage, I was unable to go into the main lobby where alcohol was being served, so I stayed in the fancy foyer of the hotel where I still got to witness the fashion show from afar. For the next two hours, I soaked up the elegance of the show, the stunning designs and the natural way the models moved and exhibited the designer clothes.

Like free wine at a wedding, the coffee was free to refill at any time and the waiter, keeping a watchful eye on how low my cup was getting, kept subtly topping it up. This ever-flowing stream of coffee, which tasted decadent at the time, also left a lasting impression, but not for the same reasons as the wheatgrass shot!

As the show came to an end, Steve came to greet me and as I stood up, I felt the blood rushing to my feet. Instantly dizzy, I tried to compose myself as we walked to his car. Driving through the busy city streets, I started getting hot and began to shake. As my mind left my body, the car sped up and I felt like I was sitting next to Lewis Hamilton, racing through the streets of Monte Carlo. Trying to compose myself, I grabbed hold of the handle of the car door and kept looking straight ahead. Be cool. BE COOL. Focusing on my breath, I tried everything I could, to stop my heart from exploding out of my chest. By the time we reached Steve's apartment, I was feeling nauseous and disorientated. Without wanting to make a scene, I excused myself, took a hot shower and went to bed.

Most of you won't have had such an extreme case of caffeine overload but, if you drink coffee regularly, particularly more than a couple of cups a day, then your body may have become resistant, meaning you 'need' more coffee to feel it's stimulating effects. Just because you don't feel like it's affecting your life, just like you don't know how great you feel when your body is hydrated, you don't know how much your body will thank you when you reduce your caffeine intake.

Caffeine is the most used psychoactive stimulant in the world and, like sugar, it can be found in some unexpected places. Too much caffeine will put pressure on your liver (which already works around

## Nutrition

the clock to absorb, digest and process your food and drink), will make you grumpy, anxious and affect your sleep patterns.

Highly addictive, and at the height of fashion with our café culture, it's no surprise that most of my clients freak out when I ask them about coffee. I get it, I'm a self-confessed tea addict so understand the emotional component behind letting go of something you love! Without giving it up entirely, reducing your caffeine content and consuming it before midday, will set you up for a better night's sleep, give your nervous system a break and overall give you more energy in the long term, not to mention make you more productive and less irritable to be around.

It's not just coffee that caffeine hides in. This addictive drug can also be found in tea (including green tea), chocolate, energy drinks, fitness-enhancing drinks and cola.

If you rely on coffee, tea, chocolate and energy drinks, how about cutting the amount you drink down by half and having your last mouthful by 12:00 pm for two weeks and see how you feel?

| How many cups of coffee/tea/caffeinated drinks I currently consume | I commit to reducing that amount down to | Results after two weeks |
| --- | --- | --- |
|  |  |  |

## Alcohol

'My husband is having a mid-life crisis and wants to run a marathon,' Christina explained. 'I've told him that under no circumstances is he doing anything so silly without the advice of a professional. Can you help?'

Her husband, Chris, was a successful entertainment lawyer, and the demanding working hours, client lunches and after-work drinks had caught up with him. Like many 40-somethings, Chris looked at his reflection one morning and decided it was time to make a change. Knowing Chris as I do now, a marathon to raise a substantial amount of money for a charity close to his heart was only ever going to be the way for him to bring back the balance of optimal health.

As I walked up to the front door of the house for our first introduction, I was struck by nerves. I was in my first eighteen months of business, and he was my first marathon client. Sitting across the table from me, it was apparent that Chris wasn't keen on the idea of a personal trainer and was only at the meeting because his wife had arranged the appointment. He was kind and friendly though and when I accepted his offer of a beer, he visibly relaxed. 'There are two things I won't do,' he said, 'And that's go to a gym and give up alcohol entirely.'

'Yep, all good. I can work with that,' I said as he relaxed further into his chair.

In the months that followed, Chris and I met twice a week, rain or shine, to get him fit and strong for his first marathon and, as the weeks continued, I noticed a change in him. Whereas before his marathon training, he had a beer or two most nights, the fitter he

## Nutrition

became and the more sponsorship that came through, the more inspired he was to do well and, as a result, the less he wanted to drink beer.

His goal became more important than having a drink or two to relax and because he had interrupted the habitual pattern, when he did decide to have a cold beer, he *chose* to rather than being at the mercy of habit.

Over time, Chris noticed his performance dropped after a night out on the beers and, as the sponsorship money rolled in and the miles increased, his commitment to the goal was reinforced. It was a no-brainer to reduce his alcohol intake.

He was listening to his body, making choices based on the bigger picture, resulting in a successful first marathon, which subsequently led him to running more and drinking less. Then he ran a second marathon two years later in New York with his family and me there for support.

No restrictions. No resentment. Aligned with values. Choice. Freedom. BOOM!

Alcohol isn't a problem. It's our relationship to it that is. Do you know why you drink? The taste? The social aspect? To give you confidence in social settings? To relax? To get hammered?

Anything we rely on and crave is an opportunity to explore the deeper issues going on beneath it. Whilst I'm not asking you to give up alcohol, I am asking you to take an honest look at how much you drink each night, how much you drink out of habit (you can't change it if you can't see it) and why you drink. Once you have the answers to these questions, you hold the power to change your relationship with alcohol. You become the master and commander of the ship rather than swimming against the tide.

> The following questions can be applied to your relationship with food, cigarettes and other substances that you rely on. Take time to answer them honestly and objectively so we can build a game plan together.
>
> My beliefs about alcohol:
> (e.g. I need a glass of wine to relax. My friends will think something is wrong with me if I don't drink. Not drinking is boring.)
>
> _____
>
> _____
>
> _____
>
> _____
>
> Alcohol gives me:
> (e.g. Peace in the moment, a moment to myself, confidence).
>
> _____
>
> _____
>
> _____
>
> _____

## Nutrition

Drinking too much alcohol stops me from:
(e.g. Getting up in the morning and exercising, spending time with the kids, being intimate with my partner).

_____

_____

_____

_____

What would happen if I reduced my alcohol intake/quit alcohol?

_____

_____

_____

What wouldn't happen if I didn't reduce my alcohol intake/quit alcohol?

_____

_____

_____

What am I pretending not to know about my relationship with alcohol?

_____

_____

_____

_____

What values do you see reflected in your answers?

_____

_____

_____

_____

## Soul food

With so much emphasis on what to eat and what not to eat, it can be easy to miss out on the joy that food brings. In many cultures, food is seen as a celebration, togetherness and community.

Rather than a chore and something that gets in the way of life, what would it be like if we adopted that same mindset? What if good, hearty, nutritious food was at the top of our priorities? What would our relationships be like if we spent more time cooking and eating together?

I understand the kick-back you might be experiencing by reading this. Thoughts like:

- 'I don't have time.'
- 'My kids/partner/flatmate are too busy.'
- 'It's just another thing for me to have to do.'

These ideas might be racing around in your mind, and fair call. Remember, nutrition is my area of weakness too, but wouldn't it be great if good nutrition was more than just food? What if nutrition was soulful, joyous and united the people we love?

Growing up, Sunday lunch, birthdays, Christmas and Easter were all cause for celebration. Those days brought the family together (and often my friends), and Mum would spend hours in the kitchen preparing delicious food for us to enjoy. Her culinary skills would put Gordon Ramsay to the test with her legendary potato salads, goulash, 'pick and choose' dish (otherwise known as paella!) and curries.

What traditions did you have growing up? Can you think of ways to create your own? If you're a busy family, it might be unrealistic to sit at the dinner table together every night, or if you are flatting, you might not cross paths too often with your roommate, but perhaps you could build in a night a week and take it in turns to cook.

Spend some time writing down what habits are stopping you from using food as a source of connection.
(e.g. eating dinner on my lap watching TV, having my phone at the table, travelling a lot for work)

_____

_____

_____

What processes will you implement to create togetherness?
(e.g. Invite friends for dinner once a month, have a family MasterChef competition, schedule a date night)

_____

_____

_____

How will this improve your relationship with food?

_____

_____

_____

_____

Nutrition

How does creating these new rituals align with your values?

_____

_____

_____

## SUMMARY AND ACTIONS

- Fuelling our body with good quality food will positively impact other areas of MENS.

- Making time to eat is essential for optimal health.

- Getting a good balance of nutrients is vital for longevity.

- We are emotional driven beings. What we eat and drink is often habitual, so interrupting the habit loop and making different choices will help change automatic responses to eating.

- You can't rely on willpower to change eating habits.

- Understand your triggers and create strategies to change your response.

- Work through the journaling prompts in this section.

'The best bridge between despair and hope is a good night's sleep.' – E. Joseph Cossman, American entrepreneur

# 9

# Sleep

So, here we are, at the S of MENS: sleep. This vital pillar of health gets pushed aside in this rat race that we are in, and it's time for that habit to change.

Your mindset, resilience and the way you see the world will change once you get your sleep hygiene in order. I understand there will be circumstances where it's not as easy. Young children, shift work and travel can all disrupt healthy patterns, but even if you adopt just some of the habits I suggest, you will still benefit.

In our modern age, we have the luxury of living around the clock. Industry benefits from this 24/7 model, but humans aren't designed to live with little sleep and now, more than ever, we are far removed from the natural cycles that keep us well. According to neuroscientist and sleep specialist, Dr Matthew Walker, author of *Why We Sleep*, on average, we sleep six hours and thirty minutes per night, which is a staggering 20 per cent less than our ancestors 100 years ago.

The idea of pulling an all-nighter to get work done and the badge of honour that comes with being able to survive on little sleep is a concerning social contagion that dramatically affects not only the quality of our lives, but our longevity too.

With all the science showing us that sleep is imperative to good health, I wonder what life would be like for you when you start prioritising sleep.

Exceptions are part of the deal in life but creating discipline and routines to give yourself the best possible chance of getting consistently good sleep, will no doubt change your life for the better.

I know the subject of sleep can be triggering for some, especially those who have tried everything, yet still lie in bed in the dark of the night tossing and turning. If this is you, I empathise and hope that some of the tips in this chapter help settle the mind.

## Tick tock, find your body clock

Circadian rhythm, translated, means 'around a day'. Our body runs on an internal clock, our sleep/wake cycle being one of them. This internal clock gets its cues from the environment, a major one being light and dark, day and night. When we are aligned, we can fall into deep and restorative sleep, consistently waking up refreshed and ready for a new day.

With the invention of electricity, and access to light at any time, humans have become out of sync with our internal body system and good quality sleep has been disrupted. Add mental and physical stress, high sugar foods and caffeine overload to the mix and our internal operating system can't function optimally.

# Sleep

Consistently poor sleep:

- Reduces our immune system
- Creates inflammation in the body
- Affects our memory
- Reduces our performance
- Affects our reproductive system
- Directly affects our mental health
- Increases our chance of injury
- Changes our ability to make decisions that align with our values

We live in a time-poor era, with the societal belief that sleep is for the weak. It begs the question: how do we bridge the gap between understanding that sleep is good for us and putting systems in place to get a good night's sleep? Knowledge isn't enough. We must apply committed action, have patience and trust the process.

I'm not at all surprised that sleep has been put to the back of the list in terms of health. It's not sexy. It's been demonised and, certainly as a society, the belief is that sleep doesn't matter.

Consider all the phrases that get thrown around and their negative connotations to sleep: 'You snooze, you lose,' 'sleeping is for the dead,' 'I'll rest when I'm dead.'

Then throw in the collective beliefs that sleeping is lazy, non-productive and a waste of life. It's no wonder that sleep hasn't been made centre stage for the world to see.

We know how difficult it can be to change behaviours, so now would be a good time to write down some of your beliefs about sleep so we can start the change process.

My beliefs about sleep:
(e.g. I've never needed much sleep. I can't sleep. I sleep better after I've had a couple of drinks. Caffeine doesn't affect my sleep.)

_____

_____

_____

How would my life be different if I slept better?

_____

_____

_____

_____

What's holding me back from sleeping well?

_____

_____

_____

## Sleep

Getting a good night sleep isn't about what you do in the last hour of the day. It's starts from the moment you wake up. Here are my top suggestions, to reset your circadian rhythm and get the good quality sleep you deserve.

### Invest in a Lumie alarm clock

Wake up with a smile on your face.

Most of us wake up to an alarm that sounds like your house is on fire. BEEP, BEEP, BEEP, BEEP. Being woken up in such an extreme way sends a rush of stress hormones through the body, which are usually met with us sitting bolt upright, ready to fight, only to realise it's just the alarm, press snooze and doze off until the same thing happens again.

This morning greeting automatically sets us up to be on high alert and sends a signal to your brain to keep a look out.

Usually what ensues is a morning 'wee', followed by picking up the phone, checking emails, messages, social media. Sometimes the emails will require action, further sending your body into fight or flight, giving other people a piece of yourself before you've even had a chance to check in to see how you are.

Once the kettle is boiled, you're onto your first hit of caffeine, relying on the hit to get you through until lunchtime, and before you know it, it's 3:00 pm, and you're reaching for coffee and sugar to give you the lift you need to get through the day.

Changing the way you wake up in the morning will literally change the trajectory of your day. We can't change our external environment, only the way we see it. Waking up naturally, without a dump of stress hormones, allows the body and mind to start the day harmoniously, and that will only make your perception of life more positive.

One way of encouraging our body to get back into its natural circadian rhythm is to use light therapy. For years now, I have used a Lumie light to wake me up instead of the ghastly alarm on my phone. Simulating sunrise and sunset, Lumie creates the perfect start and end to the day, setting me up for a good night's sleep. This works brilliantly because my natural disposition is to be 'on' from the minute I wake up. Because I wake up naturally, I have more positive and helpful thoughts and am generally a nicer human as a result!

Instead of using a Lumie light, at the very least, consider changing the tone of your alarm to one of nature, birds chirping, waterfall, for instance, something that's going to awaken your senses gradually rather than hit you for six.

Conversely, at night, instead of having all the lights on, I use the Lumie light to act as sunset (in winter) which primes my body for sleep. You could also use dimmer lights as alternatives.

## Swap your first coffee or tea of the day with water

Drink a bottle of water to rehydrate you from the night. Warm water with a slice of lemon and ginger works well to stimulate the digestive system.

## Get moving

A couple of years ago, Georgie the Labrador entered our lives, resulting in us taking her out for walks a couple of times a day. The morning walk is especially beneficial because the natural light that we are exposed to during that time helps us align with our natural body clock.

## Reduce screen time

This is easy to say and difficult to do, but screen time is overstimulating and messes with your internal clock. If you can't avoid screen time, then think about investing in blue light glasses. Blue light from our devices delays the release of melatonin, which is an essential hormone for sleep.

## Don't wait until bedtime

Greg and I had a very easy life when we first met. He kept himself busy playing semi-professional rugby and cricket. I was in the first year of my new business and neither of us had any real stress, apart from choosing what to do on our Sundays. When our first child, Jack, came along a few years later, we still had reasonably comfortable lives, albeit much busier. That all changed when we decided to move away from family and friends to start a new life in Australia. Whilst we fully understood the huge implications of packing our lives up and moving to a new country, the reality of adjusting to new time zones, getting to know a new city, dropping down to one salary and caring for two small children added to our mental load. Greg worked long hours and, by the time the kids had gone to sleep (they were three and six months at the time), there wasn't much time to talk. This resulted in bed becoming the place where the important conversations happened. Before too long, I noticed how much harder it was for me to go to sleep when we had those deeper conversations. Like watching the news at night, having exchanges about finances, work or family activated the stress response – the exact opposite response required for deep sleep.

Our rule now is to save those conversations for earlier in the day or the weekend and enjoy bed for what it's designed for – intimacy and sleep (and our funny game of stealing the other's pillow when they aren't looking)!

## Break up with your phone

I'm (almost) sure you wouldn't invite your work colleagues, friends and family into your bedroom whilst you were in your morning glory or take them with you to the toilet. Whilst I recognise that there's a big difference when they are behind a screen on an email or message, it's a good reminder to pull yourself out of the habit of taking your phone everywhere. Imagine sitting on the throne and your boss walks in to ask if you sent off the email about the important project. It's hardly going to set you up for a decent bowel movement! Or you're tucked up in bed, lights out, the phone flashes, and you see a message from your sibling moaning about your parents. It's not the relaxing environment to get the 'zzzs' you need to respond appropriately.

Leave your phone outside the bedroom (and bathroom) and, come to think of it, away from the dinner table! Phones are an instant 'being present' joy killer, which overstimulate our nervous system. As much as tech companies would like us to believe otherwise, we just aren't wired to be taking in so much information at all times. Seriously, think about the missed sleep and connection opportunities you have every day because of the attention seeking phone attached to your hand.

## Routine

Because of the big age gap between us, I was a teenager when my siblings had their children. I was the fun aunty who took any given opportunity to hang out with the gorgeous little humans. I spoiled them rotten and had first dibs on babysitting. I loved spending time with them, laughing and playing in their joyful little world. My inexperience from not having my own children meant I hyped them up by playing hide-and-seek and the tickle monster game until the sun went down and bedtime called. Fun aunty aside, they often got so hyped up, overstimulated and over-tired, the last thing they could do was settle down and get to sleep. Often, I would let them snuggle up next to me and fall asleep on the sofa whilst Des Lynam talked through the weekend's football highlights. This was great for me, but not ideal for their parents after a much needed night out!

Just as babies and children thrive from a routine to get the essential sleep hours they need, we do too. Don't underestimate the power of falling back in line with your body's natural patterns. Like seasons of the day, night time being your winter, you can unwind by giving the last hour of your day to the other humans or animals in your house through reading, bath or shower, massage or reflection.

## Overthinker? Brain dump

If you're someone who lies awake at night, turning things around in your mind, then brain-dumping might just take the edge off. Our brain wants to solve problems and, in the dark of the night, those problems seem to double in size, and before we know it, we have spiralled into a tornado of panic, throwing us deeper into darkness.

Brain dumping reassures the worrying part of your mind that you've got his back, and the beauty is that there's no thinking involved.

Simply have a notebook beside your bed, and before lights out, pick up a pen and start writing, without thought. Just let the pen guide you and gently lead you to sleep.

**Set a positive intention**

Talking of labradors earlier made me think about our mind and how it's like a loyal dog and will go and find the information we ask it to. Before you go to bed, ask yourself a positive, open-ended question and notice the difference in your mood when you wake up. Getting good quality sleep helps problem-solving, so choosing the right questions to ask and practising gratitude is quite possibly the most mood-enhancing way to start your day. Here are some ideas to ask yourself whilst you're dozing off:

- What does my body need to feel calm?
- How can tomorrow be a good day?
- How can I improve my relationship with _____?
- How do I want to feel going into tomorrow?
- How can I be of service tomorrow?
- What went well for me today and how can I apply that to tomorrow?
- What will make me feel good about my day tomorrow?

## Create the right environment

To further optimise your sleep, consider giving your bedroom a makeover. Studies have shown that creating a nurturing environment, including the right temperature, reducing noise levels, choosing sleep-enhancing colours (blues or greens) and low lighting will improve the quality of your sleep.

When we go to bed, our body temperature naturally drops, and the ideal room temperature is 18 degrees. Now, this may sound cold, but it helps to maintain the lower core level that we need in order to have a truly restful sleep.

Invest in a quality mattress that suits your constitution. We spend about a third of our lives in the comfort of our bed, so choosing the right mattress is a clever investment in your health.

## When counting sheep doesn't work

An increasing number of clients report to me that they have no issue falling asleep, but they wake up at 3:00 am and can't go back to sleep. If this sounds like you, then here are some strategies that might help:

- Count backwards from 10,000. When you get distracted, go back to the last number you remember and continue from there.
- Go through the alphabet, starting from 'A', listing things you are grateful for, beginning with that letter.
- Keep off your devices, including the television.
- Significantly reduce alcohol and caffeine.
- If you're still not asleep within twenty minutes, get out of bed, keeping the lights low. Read or do something boring and as soon as you feel sleepy, head back to bed.

## SUMMARY AND ACTIONS

- Good quality sleep might just be the most important pillar of MENS.

- Getting in sync with your circadian rhythm will promote deep sleep.

- Putting sleep off to finish important tasks is often less productive in the long run.

- Sleep hygiene starts from the moment you wake up.

- A good routine creates the right environment for sleep.

- Complete the journaling prompts in this chapter.

- Create a sleep hygiene plan that combines the other pillars in the MENS framework.

As we go through life, we will inevitably be met with challenges from internal struggles (beliefs, conflicts of values and the way we react to situations) to external stressors (environment, financial stress, draining relationships, lack of exercise, poor nutrition and sleep) that disrupt our constitution. These stressors bring dis-ease and imbalance, leaving us feeling disenchanted with life.

# 10

# Bringing It All Together with Ayurveda

Ayur-what?!

Ayurveda translates to 'the knowledge of life' and originated in India more than 5,000 years ago. This fascinating science fully aligns with my way of coaching and deserves a mention in this book.

Ayurveda takes the individual as they are and zooms out, looking at the whole picture of the individual's life instead of focusing only on the symptoms they present with. Using psychology, nutrition, movement, spirituality massage, and herbs, Ayurveda can help balance the body and mind, bringing it back to its natural balance.

The science of Ayurveda enshrines the belief that every person has their own energy pattern, a unique mix of mental, physical and emotional characteristics. As we go through life, we will inevitably be met with challenges from internal struggles (beliefs, conflicts of values and the way we react to situations) to external stressors (environment, financial stress, draining relationships, lack of exercise, poor nutrition and sleep) that disrupt our constitution. These stressors bring dis-ease and imbalance, leaving us feeling disenchanted with life.

Sattva, Rajas and Tamas are the three great qualities, or in Sanskrit 'maha gunas'. They are thought of as universal energies that exist within us and are ever-changing. They affect our mental, physical and spiritual states, so it's wise to understand how they impact us so we can bring ourselves back to balance.

**Sattva** = Balance, intelligence, bliss, awareness, wisdom, peace and freedom.

**Rajas** = Movement, energy, change, takes action, courage, and passion.

**Tamas** = Inertia, negativity, ignorance, destruction, stuck, lazy and materialistic.

Like the two wolves' story (explained in chapter 11), they live inside us, arising and passing throughout our lives. We have the choice as to which one we feed.

It's unrealistic to assume we are going to go through life stress-free. There will be times when we move into a tamastic state, so using rajas in the form of courage and action, we can pull ourselves out and back on the path to sattva.

This means: practising self-observation (mindfulness) and having a strong sense of purpose, living to your values, seeking out people and places that give you joy allows you to live in the light.

# Bringing It All Together with Ayurveda

**The elements:**

The five elements in Ayurveda exist within all of us and combine to form our constitution.

The five elements are:

- Ether
- Air
- Fire
- Water
- Earth

Ayurveda looks to bring order back to the body and restore equilibrium to the mind using three energy principles, otherwise known as doshas:

- Vata – air and space
- Pitta – fire and water
- Kapha – earth and water

We are all born with one more dominant dosha but all three exist within us. Disease and mental changes occur when one or more of these doshas are disturbed.

There is so much to say about the doshas, so I'm going to keep it simple and tell you about the qualities they display when they are in balance, what symptoms they present with, when they are out of balance, the causes and how to overcome them.

## Vata Profile:

| Governs communication and movement ||
|---|---|
| **Balanced vata** | **Imbalanced vata** |
| <ul><li>Enthusiastic</li><li>Positive</li><li>High energy</li><li>Calm mind</li><li>Creative</li><li>Friendly</li><li>Fun</li><li>Inspirational</li><li>Love change</li></ul> | <ul><li>Stressed</li><li>Depressed</li><li>Anxiety</li><li>Lonely</li><li>Insecure</li><li>Nervous</li><li>Fearful</li><li>Trouble sleeping</li><li>Dry skin</li><li>IBS symptoms</li><li>Cracking joints</li><li>Dehydration</li></ul> |
| **Causes** | **Remedy** |
| <ul><li>Over-stimulation</li><li>Over-committing</li><li>Travel and flying</li><li>Excess stress</li><li>Big life changes</li><li>Unsettled, cold and windy weather</li></ul> | <ul><li>Increase opposing qualities</li><li>Reduce workload/commitments</li><li>Meditation</li><li>Restorative yoga</li><li>Massage</li><li>Consistent daily routine</li><li>Warming foods</li><li>Warmth in general (baths, wheat bag)</li></ul> |

## Pitta Profile:

| Governs passion and metabolism | |
|---|---|
| **Balanced pitta** | **Imbalanced pitta** |
| • Positive<br>• Fun<br>• Playful<br>• Passionate<br>• Confident<br>• Charming<br>• Determined<br>• Ambitious<br>• Focused on tasks<br>• Energetic | • Heat aversion<br>• Angry<br>• Irritated<br>• Stubborn<br>• Frustrated<br>• Judgemental<br>• Intense<br>• Jealous<br>• Over-competitive<br>• Inflamed skin, acne, boils<br>• High blood pressure |
| **Causes** | **Remedy** |
| • Workaholics<br>• Putting themselves under too much pressure<br>• Demands perfection from themselves<br>• Caffeine<br>• Alcohol<br>• Spicy foods<br>• Fasting | • Reduce competition<br>• Non-competitive exercise<br>• Being out in nature<br>• Calming massage<br>• Loving kindness meditation<br>• Cooling food and drink (aloe vera, cold peppermint tea) |

## Kapha Profile:

| Governs love and structure ||
|---|---|
| **Balanced kapha** | **Imbalanced kapha** |
| <ul><li>Loving</li><li>Compassionate</li><li>Loyal</li><li>Reliable</li><li>Always there for others</li><li>Great friend</li><li>Gives good hugs</li><li>Forgiving</li><li>Good stamina</li><li>Strong</li></ul> | <ul><li>Possessive</li><li>Greedy</li><li>Lazy</li><li>Brain fog</li><li>Depressed</li><li>Mental and physical inertia</li><li>Slow</li><li>Heavy</li></ul> |
| **Causes** | **Remedy** |
| <ul><li>Sitting too much</li><li>Not moving daily</li><li>Overeating</li><li>Heavy and oily foods</li><li>Cold</li></ul> | <ul><li>Move the body with regular exercise</li><li>Dynamic movements</li><li>Deep tissue massage</li><li>Sauna</li><li>Dry body brushing</li><li>Avoid snacking, stick to three meals a day</li></ul> |

You might already see elements of yourself in these profiles and you can easily find out your dominant dosha by taking a simple test online. I recommend this one from Harmony Inspired Health. https://www.harmonyinspiredhealth.com.au/freebies/

The brilliance of this ancient system is that it allows us to detach from and re-examine ourselves through the lens of the elements

## Bringing It All Together with Ayurveda

and doshas. Instead of getting stuck in the mind, trying to change, resisting what is and blaming ourselves or others for our circumstances, Ayurveda guides us back to balance by using a simple principle. Like attracts like and opposites balance.

When I work with clients who are hooked on a story or belief, I use Ayurveda to restore equilibrium.

Karen was a client of mine who came to see me because she was feeling stressed at work and was at a crossroads in her life. She felt she had lost herself and wanted to spend some time finding herself again.

She knew she had to make some changes, but she felt scattered, overwhelmed and holding a lot of stress in her body. A natural giver, Karen spent a lot of her energy on her family, friends and work colleagues, leaving very little in the tank for herself. Highly critical of herself, she spent a lot of time in her head, overthinking past conversations, second-guessing herself and making assumptions of others based on her worldview.

Her compassionate nature meant that she got drawn into other people's drama cycles at work and this was depleting her energy further.

She wasn't fulfilled at work and felt undervalued and unappreciated. This fuelled her limiting core belief that she wasn't good enough and her negative self-talk was at an all-time high.

Her waking and sleeping routines were erratic and, like many of us, she used technology long into the night and reached for her phone first thing in the morning. She was conscious of the fact that she wasn't making time for exercise and wanted to get outside more. Her diet was hit-and-miss.

Karen was displaying a kapha and vata imbalance, so the first thing we focused on was reducing the stress in her body by establishing a good routine.

For the first couple of weeks, she cultivated the discipline of going to bed and waking up at the same time. She did this through the following strategies:

- Going for a walk straight after work
- Reducing her tech time
- Spending one-on-one time with her son
- Not pressing snooze on her alarm
- Taking five big intentional breaths before getting out of bed
- Not checking her phone for the first 30 minutes of waking.
- Becoming aware of her repetitive thoughts and writing them down
- Treating herself with compassion as she uncovered the nature of her inner critic

As the weeks progressed, Karen's disposition changed. She started to see herself in a more positive light. Her body language changed, and she was able to unhook from the negative self-talk and negativity at work. Instead of being drawn into the toxic environment, she used her values to step above the line and remove herself from the low-level energy.

Each week, we added simple mindset, physical and spiritual tasks, layering them over the previous weeks, so by the end of our time together, she had built a solid foundation to work from.

The stability of the routine she created increased her energy levels, which built momentum, confidence and clarity. For the first time in years, she could see a way out. Six months on, Karen has lost 14 kg in weight, walks every day, has changed career and she's feeling the best she's felt in years. Thanks, Ayurveda! That will do nicely.

## A word from Karen

*The life coaching sessions with Anna were a godsend for me during a time of uncertainty, self-doubt, low self-esteem and feeling like a constant failure.*

*These feelings and thoughts took over my whole being without even realising it. This caused a lot of constant 'monkey-chatter' in my head, and it drove me to reach out for help.*

*I often go back through my notes to see how far I have come after seeing Anna over the course of 12 weeks.*

*Anna was 'real' and didn't sugar-coat anything, which I responded to. It was good to have a 'real' talk about stuff.*

*I have since:*

- *Quit my stressful job and found one that I enjoy*
- *Leapt out of bed at 5.30 am for a half-hour power-walk*
- *Given up alcohol*
- *Lost 14 kgs*

*None of this would have happened if I hadn't invested in some time with Anna.*

## Dinacharya

Dinacharya is a daily routine that maintains physical health and promotes optimal health and wellbeing. I love this part of Ayurveda because it speaks volumes about the importance of a good, consistent and positive routine.

Dinacharya promotes moderation, routine and living in tune with our circadian rhythm. No deprivation, extreme living, just simple, self-care to enhance wellbeing and happiness.

Building a healthy routine can help keep the doshas in balance, create energy, focus and clarity.

The morning practices are designed to induce energy and calmness within the body. Less of the tired and wired constitution, and instead focusing on optimising rajas and sattva.

Some of these routines may feel odd to start with, but like anything new, have the discipline to give it fair trial, experiment for a few weeks, notice any changes and then make your mind up if it suits you or not.

Some of these practices may be unrealistic for you to regularly implement, so modify them to suit your lifestyle. I recommend tongue scraping to all of my clients. They all come back with similar feedback:

- I have improved taste
- Some of the sugary foods I used to enjoy, don't do it for me anymore
- I don't have bad breath anymore
- My mouth feels cleaner

## Bringing It All Together with Ayurveda

Check out the list below and mark the activities you will try for the next four weeks:

> **Dinacharya**
>
> **I commit to**
>
> - Wake up when the sun rises (or use Lumie alarm)
> - Wash my face
> - Tongue scrape with a tongue scraper (copper)
> - Brush teeth
> - Sip herbal tea or warm lemon water
> - Elimination of bladder and bowels
> - Self-massage to stimulate lymphatic flow
> - Five big deep breaths in and out of the nose or five minutes' meditation
> - Yoga (sun salutations) or a walk in nature
> - Shower
> - Breakfast

Developing your own morning routine sets you up for the day ahead and puts the ball in your court. Rather than being at the mercy of others from the moment you get out of bed, Dinacharya gives you time to yourself to deeply connect. This sends a powerful message out to the world that you are ready for what's to come today.

Even if you choose a handful of these suggestions, you will notice a positive change in your constitution.

One of the things I love most about Ayurveda is that, like its sister, yoga, it gives us permission to get out of our head and into our body. We can connect to our deeper self, our intuition, our soul.

## Only Human

This might sound out the gate and too "woo woo", but it's when we cut out the noise, release the ego and go inside where we find the good stuff.

We can let go of the stress we thought was important, stop living like we are on *The Truman Show* and enjoy a life we truly deserve.

It's in this place, outside of our thinking brain, where we can create a safe mindset. When we feel safe, we can tolerate change. When we tolerate change, we don't repeat old habits and we start getting the results we want.

You have nothing to lose by giving these ancient techniques a go. Treat it like an experiment for four weeks. Be the curious scientist. You might just be surprised at what you discover.

An old Cherokee teaches his grandson about life. 'A fight is going on inside me,' he says to the boy. 'It is a terrible fight and it is between two wolves. One is evil – he is anger, envy, sorrow, regret, greed, arrogance, self-pity, guilt, resentment, inferiority, lies, false pride, superiority and ego.'

The wise old man continued, 'The other is good – he is joy, peace, love, hope, serenity, humility, kindness, benevolence, empathy, generosity, truth, compassion and faith. The same fight is going on inside you – and inside every other person, too.'

The grandson thought about it for a minute, and then asked his grandfather, 'Which wolf will win?'

The old Cherokee simply replied, 'The one you feed.'

# 11

# It's in Your Hands

An old Cherokee teaches his grandson about life. 'A fight is going on inside me,' he says to the boy. 'It is a terrible fight and it is between two wolves. One is evil – he is anger, envy, sorrow, regret, greed, arrogance, self-pity, guilt, resentment, inferiority, lies, false pride, superiority and ego.'

The wise old man continued, 'The other is good – he is joy, peace, love, hope, serenity, humility, kindness, benevolence, empathy, generosity, truth, compassion and faith. The same fight is going on inside you – and inside every other person, too.'

The grandson thought about it for a minute, and then asked his grandfather, 'Which wolf will win?'

The old Cherokee simply replied, 'The one you feed.'

The process of writing this book has reinforced in my own mind just how important the MENS framework is to success.

Being a deeply introspective person, with a strong desire to help positively change lives, this undertaking had me waking in the middle of the night, with anxiety about delivering the best material I could for my readers. This unconscious fear made me hyper-focused, serious and, at times, hard to live with. I often felt sick and would spend hours staring at the screen, wondering how I was going to articulate my message. It was tempting not to eat. One night, I woke up at 2am and decided it would be a good idea to write all night, only to work a full day of clients the next day.

There was something romantic about writing under the stars whilst the rest of the country slept soundly, but the reality was that it set me back three days from the exhaustion that hit me later! I didn't make it to the gym as much, but I did make myself take the dog out for a walk. I'll be honest, though, the voice of a tyrant in my head told me I was slacking. There were days when I felt so low that I didn't believe my own words. But then I reminded myself which wolf to feed and directed myself back to the basics of MENS.

As this book draws to a close, I want to remind you of a few things:

## Take care of the basics:

- Taking care of your basic needs will transform your life. It's *that* important. You will no doubt drift back into old habits so, be vigilant, curb the excuses and get back to task as soon as you notice you've slipped.

- Create easy systems to implement change.

- Anticipate your roadblocks and accept they are inevitable. Have an unwavering mindset to maintain a high level of self-care.

- Fatigue and negativity will challenge your discipline. Be aware of these traps and challenge the negative self-talk. Feed the right wolf.

## Know your values:

- Creating change is hard. Use your values to guide you home.

- Be more than you believe you are – BECOME the person you aspire to be by changing your behaviour.

- Live courageously and choose hard over easy when you need to.

- Disengage from other people's opinions and look 'within' for the right answers for YOU.

- Live simply, avoid drama.

Memento mori is Latin for 'remember that you must die'.

Guys, this life is it. It's your life, and it's the only one you will ever have. You have one shot to live it well. So, how are you going to play it?

Waiting for tomorrow to change or take the risks to better your life is a day too late.

Make those changes now and do it with passion and purpose.

Looking after yourself is the biggest gift you can give yourself AND others. When you find a system that works for you, commit wholeheartedly to adhering to it so you can show up to your life with 100 per cent intent.

You owe it to yourself, and you owe it to your loved ones too. There's nothing selfish about being the best version of yourself and sharing that with the world. If you've been putting it off, now's the time to put the gloves on and go get it.

## Find the joy

Joy is a whole book in itself. I can't stress enough the importance of joy and connection in living a good life.

Laugh, please, and find the people who make you laugh. Actively seek out joy. Encourage your inner child. Look for the moments to connect with the others who bring out the playful, carefree spirit in you. Life doesn't have to be so serious. Make this a priority and watch your relationships transform.

## Find your tribe

Loneliness is real and our mental and physical health is suffering because of it. Connection and the importance of it is weaved throughout this book and I want to reinforce how damaging it can be if you let your relationships slip.

Make the time to catch up with the people that matter. Schedule the call. Block out your diary for social engagement. Seek out the people that lift you up, support you and do the same for them.

I understand you have commitments. I understand you are busy. But our modern-day stressors aren't going away anytime soon, so make your interactions with others a priority. You won't regret it.

## Keep doing the work

The work of being 'better than I was yesterday' is never done. There's no top of the mountain. Our mind is a complex web. Our beliefs and fears are deeply committed to keeping us safe. Our ego is on the hunt for threats. It is your responsibility to choose which wolf to feed.

Be your own hero. Look up to yourself and do hard things well. Do this, and your life will undoubtedly change. But remember not to put too much pressure on yourself. This work is about being comfortable with where you are and being courageous enough to know how to move towards positively aligning with your values. If you feel pressured, it is most likely coming from a place of lack: unworthiness, mistrust and fear.

Being connected to your values, knowing your self-worth, and pursuing a life that aligns with what truly matters to you will bring you home.

This is just the beginning for you. I've set the framework, and it's now over to you to create the processes, gather your support network, get clear on what you want out of life and go for it with full passion and commitment.

The work starts now, and I'm here to help you keep up the momentum. Utilise the additional free content I've provided for you and keep this book in plain sight. Use it as your daily guide and don't lose track of your vision.

## Only Human

All the resources are yours to help keep you inspired and motivated.

Be a changemaker who inspires change in others.

Live MENS like your life depends on it – because it does.

Above all else, remember, you're ONLY HUMAN.

# Acknowledgements

I would like to thank my family, friends and clients who supported me in writing this book. Without their belief in me, this book would still be in my head.

Thanks to my husband, Greg, and kids, Jack and Sienna, for standing by me through thick and thin – a constant support, especially on the days when it all got too hard.

To the key people who read, gave feedback and encouragement to make this book as good as it could be before it went to print. Thank you!

To Dale Radford, who sponsored this project, thank you for supporting my dreams to reach more people. Your contribution means the world to me.

And finally, a huge thank you to my clients and to you, the readers, for trusting in my words, for standing shoulder-to-shoulder with me and for taking the courageous first steps towards positive change.

# References

Edith Eger – *The Choice*
James Clear – *Atomic Habits*
Charles Duhigg – *The Power of Habit*
Matthew Walker – *Why We Sleep*
Michael Moss – *Salt, Sugar, Fat* and *Hooked*
Harmony Robinson-Stagg – Ayurvedic and Integrative Health Practitioner
Henry Fraser – Mouth artist and author
Aaron Beck – CBT Triangle formula
Russ Harris – *ACT Made Simple*
Dr James Gordon – *The Lemon Visualisation*
Dan Carter- The High-Performance Podcast

Photo credits:
**Salina Galvan Photography**
**P: + 64 (0) 21 185 5401**
**facebook.com/salinagalvanphotography**

# About the Author

Anna Veale is the founder of Fresh Coaching, a mindset and bodyworks consultancy specialising in men's mental fitness. She started her career as a personal trainer and sports massage therapist in 2003 before transitioning into the life coaching industry in 2018. Anna's absolute commitment to the wellbeing of others has made her a leader in her industry, with clients ranging from top sportsmen to business leaders. The results speak volumes.

As a professional member of the Australia and New Zealand Coaching Alliance (ANZCAL), Anna is always seeking out opportunities to upskill to ensure she has the most up-to-date and relevant skills to offer her clients.

Originally from England, Anna lives in the beautiful coastal city of Tauranga, New Zealand, with her husband and two children.

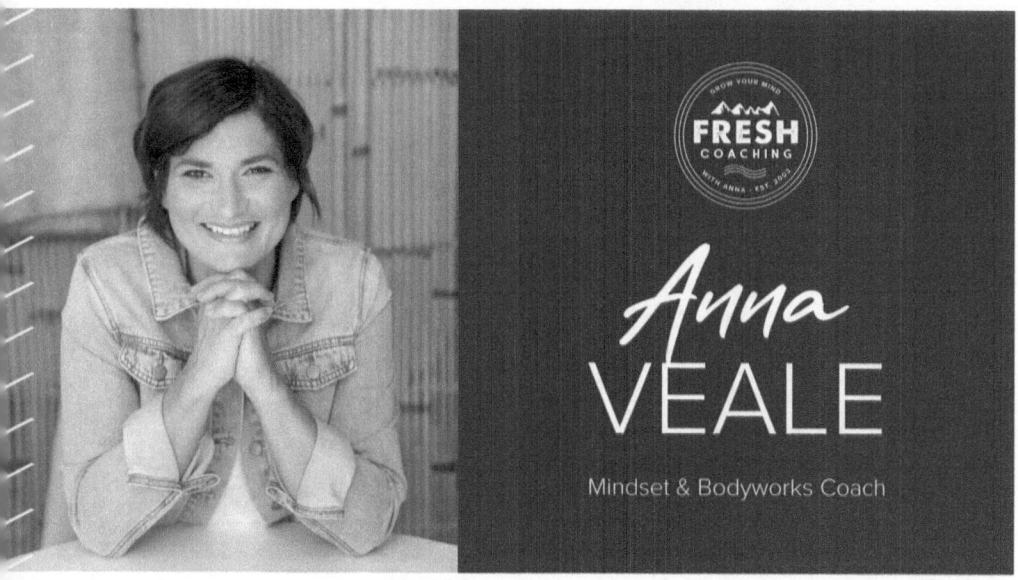

**Anna Veale is a mindset and bodyworks coach specialising in men's mental fitness and the author of 'Only Human'.**

She started her career as a Personal Trainer and Sports Massage Therapist in 2003 before transitioning into the Mindset Coaching Industry in 2018. Her extensive work with professional athletes, business owners and Leaders has led her to run workshops and events around New Zealand and The United Kingdom. An engaging and easy going speaker, Anna easily connects with her audiences and often receives feedback that she just 'gets it'. She is available for online and in-person speaking events, workshops and 1-1 coaching and can cater per presentation and topic to any audience.

**Her three signature talks are:**

IT'S ALL IN YOUR HEAD

- Identify and defuse negative and unhelpful thoughts
- Promote self-awareness, increase happiness, well-being and acceptance of life as it is
- Learn simple daily techniques to break the habitual thought cycle that causes anxiety, unrest, and disease.

STRESS BUSTING SOLUTION

- Identify stress, the various disguises it wears and understand its impacts
- Get clear on your values so you can confidently set boundaries and reduce the mental load at work and at home.
- Reduce chronic stress, which can negatively impact your health, relationships, and productivity.

MAN UP

- Learn the MENS formula. Use it to clean up your habits and get on top of your health
- Re-evaluate your work-life balance
- Increase confidence and transform your life

## Get in touch

To enquire about engaging Anna to speak at your next event, email freshcoachingnz@gmail.com or call **027 521 3789**

 @freshcoachingnz    @annavealecoach   www.freshcoaching.me

# Access to Free Resources

http://www.freshcoaching.me/onlyhumanresources

# Testimonials

I have been working with Anna from Fresh Coaching for over two years and over that time, she has given me the tools and strategies to be able to cope with 'the black dog'. Anna's approach is both gentle knowledge-based and practical, which gives me the perfect balance to work through my issues and be able to not only live again but thrive in the world!

**Stacey Roche, Paralympian**

I have known Anna and her family for around 10 years. So, when I was facing obstacles in my life, I decided to use her professional services, to supply me with the tools and resources to build my bridge and get over it, and on with my life. After her help, I have not looked back, excelling in my chosen sport again and looking at my life and choices in a different, more positive way than before.

**Robbie McNair**

In my current role as Director of Football at Otumoetai FC, we have used Anna on a few occasions to work with our players and coaches on delivering mindset and mental skills workshops. Anna has a wealth of knowledge and experiences that she is able to share with the groups and is also great at pitching to the audience, working with male and female athletes of different ages to make a real difference to their performance, on and off the field. I would highly recommend Anna and look forward to continuing to work with her and Fresh Coaching in the future!

**Joe Dixon, Director of Sport Otumoetai Football Club**

For the past two years, Anna has been working as a Health and Wellness Consultant with our staff. This role has had multiple facets, including group workshops as well as individual one-on-one coaching, to ensure our staff are happy and productive in both their working and non-working life. Having a direct service that staff can utilise, either regularly or as required, depending on need, has taken a significant amount of pressure off us as business owners attempting to work in an area we are not experienced in and have little time to address. It has also been great to support our staff to live fulfilling lives and support them during tough times. With Anna being independent from us, I believe it is a huge strength as staff are comfortable discussing all topics confidentially. As required, points are then used in group discussions with management, to ensure we are supporting our staff to achieve their goals and continue to develop their potential.

**Jacinta Horan, Bureta Physiotherapy + Wellness NZ**

## Testimonials

As a fellow coach and facilitator, I happily recommend Anna. Anna did a Masterclass for Australia and New Zealand Coaching Alliance earlier this year (2021). She was very professional to deal with and her resources were professionally presented. The Masterclass followed a very good structure and format and was incredibly informative. Anna is fabulous. She is personable, passionate about helping people (particularly men and their health) and really knows her stuff. She is also very professional, while being real, and can (and will) adapt to you and your style.

**Christine Walter**
**High Performance Certified mBIT Coach, Certified NLP Trainer Certified mBIT Trainer and Business Owner ANZCAL**

Six months ago, I hit a really low point in my life, with a bad break up, struggling with my career and had lost complete confidence in myself. A life coach had been suggested to me by a family member and, after our first phone call, I already felt that Anna was going to guide me out of this tough point in my life. Opening up for me was uncomfortable and a bit difficult, at times, but Anna would quickly put me at ease and made the experience really enjoyable and fun and made my qualities and values clear to me. She helped me to break down trouble areas in my life and pushed me to set goals and go for them. In my time with Anna life literally just changed so quickly, I had the confidence to nail a really good job, got back into my fitness and back into the things I enjoy with a positive mindset. I cannot thank Anna enough for her help and support and would recommend this experience to everyone.

**Russell, Manawatu, NZ**

Anna is an amazing person with a gift that helped me climb over some huge mountains, in both my personal and work life. Through looking at my values, I have gained an understanding of my true potential, to enhance who I am and be able to achieve my goals and ambitions.

Anna has given me life-changing tools to help me change negative and discouraging thoughts and patterns into focus and drive, taking my life in a positive direction.

**Braedon, Tauranga, NZ**


At the most challenging time of my life, I was offered Anna's details by a friend. I had not spoken to anyone professionally or even considered it previously. I made contact and we spoke weekly for six weeks. Anna helped guide me through this period by asking questions that made me be honest with myself about what I wanted and how I could get there. She gave me the confidence to make some life-changing decisions and really move forward.

**Russell, Auckland, NZ**

# Offers

Game time

You've read the book. You feel inspired. Here are some ways to help you get the results you want before you settle back into your familiar, unhelpful habits.

## MENS quiz and e-book

I've created a quiz to help you determine where to start in improving your health, so you get the results you want.

Upon completion, you will be sent an easy-to-follow playbook which will keep you accountable and motivated to stick to tasks.

# Offers

## Book me for your next event

More and more guys are realising the importance of connection for mental wellbeing and are creating opportunities to catch up and talk. Be it online or face-to-face, I can support you by taking you through one of my signature, informal workshops or teach you more about the magic of breathwork and yin yoga.

## The habit changer

If you're ready for the real deal and want to take full responsibility for your life moving forward, the habit changer session is for you.

Take advantage of 50% off this thirty-minute express call where Anna will nail down the basics of habit change so you can start embedding new pathways and get the positive results you are looking for.

These spaces are limited so get in quickly to secure your call.

# Notes

www.ingramcontent.com/pod-product-compliance
Lightning Source LLC
Chambersburg PA
CBHW030259100526
44590CB00012B/443